THE DEDALUS PRESS

editor John F. Deane

Charlie Donnelly
The Life and Poems

by
JOSEPH DONNELLY

THE DEDALUS PRESS
46 Seabury, Sydney Parade Avenue, Dublin 4. Ireland.

© "Life" and Poems, Joseph Donnelly 1987

ISBN 0 948268 30 1 (paper)
ISBN 0 948268 31 X (bound)

The Dedalus Press receives financial assistance
from the Arts Council/An Chomhairle Ealaíon, Ireland.

Typesetting, Make-up and Printing by The Nationalist, Carlow.

Cover design by Brendan Foreman based on an original cover design by
Rosemarie Donnelly.

CONTENTS

INTRODUCTION 7

THE LIFE
Chapter One 11
Chapter Two 17
Chapter Three 25
Chapter Four 35
Chapter Five 48

THE POEMS
On First Hearing John Court McCormack 59
Da Mihi 60
The Death Song 61
To You 62
At the Dreaming of the Dreams 63
The Professor 64
To a Bad Critic 65
The Dead 66
In a Library 67
Stasis 68
Small Birds Seen through Tenuous Trees 69
Approach 70
Mr. Sheridan's Morning Prayer 71
Story 72
Music, Nice Turns of Thought 73
Wages of Deviation 74
Unnoticed in Hurry of Callous Good-Bye 75
The Flowering Bars 76
The Tolerance of Crows 77
Poem 78
Heroic Heart 79
Fragments, 1, 2, 3 80

Notes on the Poems 81

Ewart Milne: Song of the Night Market 83
Ewart Milne: Thinking of Artolas 84
Cecil Ffrench Salkeld: Soccoro Rojo 87
Blanaid Salkeld: Casualties 88
David Clarke: Vindication 89
Donagh MacDonagh: Charles Donnelly 90

Charlie Donnelly, 1936, prior to his departure for Spain.

INTRODUCTION

The publication of this Memoir concludes a chapter in my life which began during the summer of 1967 when I found myself in hospital with a serious illness.

The life and death of my brother, Charlie, had always been an influence in my life, even unconsciously and before I realised his importance as a poet. But by 1967 immediate memories of him had faded as life had assumed a normal pattern — business, marriage, family.

The nineteen-sixties, in hindsight, was a period of significant change world-wide. A new post-war generation was beginning to emerge. Spurred on by a new liberalism in political, social and religious thought, young students were again taking to the streets.

Reports of unrest and demonstrations from many centres in the world, especially France, awakened memories of the 1930's which had continued through to the fifties were being challenged.

A thought crystallised in my mind — Charlie's story should be told, he should be remembered.

How this could be done was another matter but the idea persisted. It was reinforced and enlarged when I attended, in early 1968, a memorial presentation of the life and works of the late Donagh MacDonagh in the Abbey Threatre. Here I first heard MacDonagh's poem, "Charlie Donnelly, Dead in Spain", in tribute to Charlie and was deeply moved. Memories came flooding back of the whole sad episode.

I learnt from my brother, Paul, who was living in America at that time, that there was a reference to Charlie and his poetry in a book, The Lincoln Battalion, by Edwin Rolfe, which was a history of the Abraham Lincoln Battalion. Through a friend, Wm. Durkan, I got a copy of the book and for the first time, read the two poems quoted in the book, 'Poem' and 'The Tolerance of Crows'.

Realising that the only mementoes of Charlie in the family were a few poetry books and family photographs and that my father and family, apart from my older brother, Tom, knew nothing of Charlie's poetic output, I decided to contact people who had known him in Spain and at home.

My first contact was the late Frank Edwards, who, in turn put me in touch with Brian O'Neill, late of the Irish Press and so I went on. I was impressed with Brian's insight into Charlie's character as I had been suprised at how little was known about him by most of those to whom I spoke.

Brian suggested that a Memoir would be the best means of those to whom I spoke.

Brian suggeted that a Memoir would be the best means of remembering Charlie and when I asked him to undertake the project, he amazed me by suggesting that I should do it myself. I demurred, having no illusions about myself as a writer. Brian cast aside my objections saying 'You must write as this cannot be done without you as you know the family background.' With his encouragement, I set down some of my memories on paper and submitted them to Brian and his wife, Eileen, both of whom approved.

About this time I also talked to the late Peadar O'Donnell, who read my first attempt and encouraged me saying 'You have both sides of the coin but you must do something before you burn out'. He was willing to contribute but future events prevented this.

George Gilmore was delighted to know that something was to be done to commemorate Charlie. He visited me and gave me the original of Charlie's last letter home which Tom has given to him years before. Later, in a letter, he advised me to 'emphasise the poet'.

It was obvious that without the story of Charlie's roots, it would be impossible to portray a complete picture in earlier attempts to publish his poetry and writings in the late thirites. My brother Tom, had collected whatever material Donagh MacDonagh had in his possession and had passed it on to Montague Slater who had made a collection of my brother's work for publication, but nothing came of it. In turn, Slater passed the collection to Leslie Daiken, who tried to have it published with Browne & Nolan in 1941 but they showed no interest, possibly because of the political climate at the time. Subsequently, Daiken sent a Memoir with poetry and writings to Devin Adair, New York where it remained unpublished for over thirty years before its return to me in 1970.

However, pressure of business and family commitments prevented any significant progress in producing the Memoir over the next few years, although my research continued.

In the meantime, interest in Charlie had been aroused and my failure to publish was sometimes miscontrued in some quarters. I came under pressure to publish the poems (the collection of which was not complete at the time). I believed that this was not appropriate without a Memoir although I was pleased to permit publication of individual poems in various anthologies over the years, as requested. In the meantime, I had taken out Letters of Administration to protect my brother's work.

I am not satisfied that all of Charlie's work has been collected and I intend to continue my research in some uptapped areas.

Throughout my research, I discovered, happily, that all I knew instinctively and from memory of my brother, was reinforced and confirmed in his own writings. However, on the other hand, most of what had been written about him in various anthologies and books had been understandably but irritatingly incorrect and mis-leading. Hence, this Memoir has been written to establish the basic facts of my brother's life so as to open the way for others to make a more detailed and scholarly study.

History will not record the decade of the 1930's as one of enlightenment but it was remarkable for its idealism. This idealism was best expressed in the commitment of those who went to the defence of the Spanish Republic in their fight against Fascism.

In the aftermath of the War, some were to pay a high price for their involvement, regardless of whether they came from the East or the West, for wherever a man stands for justice, if the Right don't crucify him, the Left will, or if he happens to be born into a society like ours, there will always be a fox to rob him of his good name.

I want to acknowledge the help, especially of my wife, Kay, without whom the research and compilation of this work would not have been possible. In addition to those already mentioned, I should like to thank the following for their help in various ways. All members of my family; also Erna McKenna-Donnelly, Eilis Ryan, Mrs. B. Edwards, Jack Jones, late of The Irish Press, Mrs. Rooney, Dr. Tom Hughes, the late Charlie Harkin, Desmond Greaves, Paul O'Dwyer, New York; Paul Burns, New York; the late Ed. Flaherty, New York; Peter O'Connor, Waterford; Joe Monks, London; Niall Sheridan, Cyril Cusack, the late Ewart Milne; Pauline Green, Toronto, Canada; staff of the British Library, the National Library, Dublin; Trinity College, Dublin; Fr. Michael Paul Gallagher, S.J. and Mr. Joseph O'Connor, and many others.

I would like to dedicate this book to my family.

JOSEPH DONNELLY, DUBLIN, 1987.

Charlie's birthplace: Killybrackey, Co. Tyrone.

CHAPTER ONE

> "Death comes in quantity from solved
> Problems on maps, well-ordered dispositions,
> Angles of elevation and direction."

The lines quoted above are from "The Tolerance of Crows", one of the last poems written by my brother Charlie. At the time of his death in Spain, I was in boarding school in Dundalk with my twin brothers, Peter and Paul. It wasn't until I came home for the Easter holidays that I found out my elder brother was dead. We came home at lunchtime; all through lunch my father was very quiet, and when the meal was over he called us aside, saying he had something to tell us about Charlie.

"What about Charlie?" I asked.

My father looked straight at me, and said:

"Charlie was killed fighting with the government forces in Spain." He continued talking, but I heard nothing else. All I wanted to do was to leave the room. I went out, into the sittingroom and sat down on the piano stool, in tears. After a while, my father came in, and tried to console me.

"Charlie is with your mother now," he said, reminding me of my mother's death, exactly ten years to the day before Charlie's. I listened as he went on, but all I could think or say was, "He'll pay for this". My father asked me what I meant, and I said "Franco". He looked at me with just a trace of a smile:

"And what could you do?"

I stood up, and with all the anger at Charlie's death burning inside me I said "I'll go to Spain".

At that he became serious again; he told me:

"Don't let that thought take root. 'Vengeance is mine, says the Lord, I shall repay.' Leave Franco to God. Besides, when people go to war, this kind of thing is inevitable. Charlie knew exactly what he was doing. This is a cruel world. It was cruel to Charlie, but it's all over for him now. He's with your mother; we have to live on. I have only a few years left, and you'll get a few more. Eternity is what matters. You hit that, you hit everything".

As his eyes were beginning to match mine, he turned and left the room, leaving me with his thoughts. He would never get over Charlie's death, and neither, in a sense, would I.

We were originally a Northern family, from County Tyrone, and Charlie was born in the house my grandfather built in Killybrackey, just outside Dungannon, on the 10th of July, 1914. Charles Patrick Donnelly was named after his grandfather, who was a mild man and very well read. My father always said he should have been a teacher rather than a farmer, as he had more the mind of a philosopher than a businessman. He had earned the respect of all his neighbours, both Protestant and Catholic, because of his rational tolerance. Indeed, the socialising or 'ceidhleing' that went on in my grandparents' home was such that one could hear "The Croppy Boy" or "The Sash My Father Wore" all taken in good heart by the same company. My grandmother, on the other hand, was the ambitious one. She believed in hard work and frugal living. These characteristics were to come out in all her children, especially in my father. These two had a very special game; nothing would ever pass the door but a price would have to be put on it. On one occasion, when a special pony and trap passed, he became very excited and ran to tell his mother. When he asked if they would ever have one like it, my grandmother gathered him up in her arms and said, "When you grow up, we will have a far better one".

As he grew up, it became evident that he had a great talent for buying and selling, and as time went by, more and more of the trading was left to him, with my grandfather's blessing.

With his common sense and fine judgement, he came to the attention of a local solicitor, who offered to train him for the legal profession. My grandparents agreed, with the stipulation that he be free for all fair days. After some months, it became evident that a choice would have to be made, as the burden of his legal studies and farm duties was proving too much for him and his health was beginning to suffer. A decision was made in favour of farming and cattle trading, and he went on to build a fine reputation. Some years later, at a cattle fair in Dungannon, he bought a cow from a young farmer, which at the time seemed to be a real bargain. But the next morning, the cow took ill and died. So he went to see the young farmer, to make good his loss. The farmer was surprised at the story, but agreed to put things right. They then went inside for a cup of tea, where my father first set eyes on Rose McCaughey. Within a short time they were married, and my grandfather passed on the ownership of Killybrackey House to the young married couple.

This, then, was the sort of family that Charlie was born into. He was a bright child, and was well loved by all, especially by his great-aunt, Sarah Ann Begley. Charlie soon displayed his intelligence as he took advantage of poor Sarah Ann. She would visit him often, and bring him for walks. On one of these walks, Charlie asked to be brought to the piggery, well knowing that Sarah Ann had no fondness for pigs. She agreed, however, and brought him. When they got there, she lifted him up to see the pigs over the half door, but this wasn't good enough for Charlie, who wanted to go in. Reluctantly, she pulled the bar to open the door, whereupon Charlie said "Ladies first", and as she went inside, Charlie closed and locked the gate behind her. All her pleading was in vain, Charlie was enjoying himself! Still only concerned for the child, she warned him not to go near the well. This was a second fatal mistake, for Charlie immediately announced his intention of going there straight away and informed my great aunt, "You can't stop me now!" All the commotion, however, brought my mother from the house, who soon sorted things out. My father, when he heard the story, was greatly amused, saying that the boy wasn't slow and would have a great future.

Charlie was a sensitive boy. Once when my father was returning home late from a business trip, he had an accident. His pony took fright when it saw the light of an on-coming vehicle and he was thrown over a hedge into a field. Fortunately, he wasn't injured and, with the help of the other party involved, managed to get his pony and trap back on the road. When he got home, he told my mother what had happened, and she told him that Charlie had asked them all to say the Rosary for his Daddy, at about the time of the accident.

My grandfather died in 1917, and this gave my father the freedom to expand his horizons a little. He was thinking of buying a larger farm nearby. It was over 100 acres of good land and was held by Protestants. At the auction, my father put in the last bid which was £300.00. short of the reserve. As an encouragement, a number of his Protestant friends offered to make up the difference. However, my father was swayed by the arguments of his Uncle, Barney Begley, who resented his leaving the old home. But the underlying reason was the inconvenience his Uncle would be caused if he were to leave the neighbourhood, as my father helped him on fair days. Later on, despite his uncle's objections, he decided to sell the house and leave Dungannon.

The farm was sold to neighbours. The family moved to Dundalk where my father satisfied another ambition by opening a shop. He bought some land outside Dundalk, so that he could continue his cattle trading. He also acquired some property. His sisters, Lizzie and Minnie had already moved to Dundalk where they too had opened a shop. From now on he was to make real progress. These were happy day for my parents. The shop was very successful and he was now really getting on in the world. His progress did not go unnoticed in the community and by 1920, during the War of Independence, he was well established and admired as a man of his word.

During this period, a dispute arose with one of his tenants which led to court proceedings. The tenant insisted on attending a Sinn Fein court. My father agreed and arrangements were duly made. At the hearing, my father conducted his own defence. The representatives of the new State listened patiently and gave him the verdict. He had not expected to come off so well, but, as he talked to these men, he realised that they were honest, reasonable men of his own class and standards.

Charlie was sent to the Christian Brothers' School. He was a quick learner and my parents were very proud of him. Remembering how he had learnt about trading from his mother, my father started bringing Charlie to the local fairs. On one such trip to the fair, at about the age of seven, Charlie observed my father buying some cattle early on and then selling them again for a handsome profit. This greatly puzzled Charlie and he asked my father, "How can they be worth more over here than they were over there?" This was a strange remark to my father, and an unsettling one, for it questioned his whole way of life. As was often to be the case with Charlie's questions, he had no ready answer but went to ask a priest friend of his. The priest missed the deep nature of the question and reassured my father with the words: "No one goes to the fair for fresh air. You go with your eyes open, or you shouldn't be there". But that sort of questioning would be the source of much pain to both of them in the future.

With the signing of the Treaty in 1921, the War of Independence came to an end. The Civil War which followed created new hatreds, but little else. My father's sympathies were with Collins and Griffith and he supported the government of W. T. Cosgrave. However, this period was to have little effect on our family as my father's main preoccupation in life was his family and business, not politics. Indeed, when he found that one of Charlie's teachers, a staunch Republican, was inflicting his views on the boys in class, he went straight to the principal to tell him that he wasn't sending his son to school to be taught politics. In his view, politics should be left to the politicians and, in any case, he would endorse Dean Swift's judgement that 'the man who sowed two blades of grass where formerly there was one, served his country best.'

Unwittingly, on one occasion he became involved with the IRA. By 1924 he had bought a car, a Ford Model T. There were few cars in the area at the time and one day two strangers came into the shop and asked to hire the car to make a short journey across the border; they offered a fee of £5. My father agreed and undertook the journey. It is worth noting that he could travel anywhere in the border districts without question as he was well known. When they reached their destination, he realised that he was in an IRA camp and was dealing with the 'Irregulars'. On the return journey he began to realise the dangerous position he could have been in, had he been stopped by the authorities and his passengers searched. He promised himself that he would not be used this way again; soon after this incident, he sold the car.

As the family was growing larger, my parents decided to build a new home on the outskirts of Dundalk, away from the shop and the business. Work began in the summer of 1926 and was finished in February 1927 just as my youngest sister, Carmel, was born. Within a couple of weeks of Carmel's birth, my mother decided that she would buy a new suit for Charlie for his Confirmation and, at the same time, have a little outing after her confinement. While on this outing, she picked up an infection and developed a streptococcal throat. I was sent away to the country with Charlie to friends of my father's during my mother's illness. After a couple of days, a stranger called in a car to take Charlie away. I was told he was going to school. Little I knew that the end had come for my mother. I was unhappy now as I felt alone, but after a few days my father and Charlie returned to take me home.

I was very happy to see them and asked Charlie to take a walk with me in the fields to see my new friends, the animals. After I had introduced him to the chickens, hens and cattle, he mentioned my mother, and so, on bended knee, he came level with me and told me that Mammy had gone to heaven. I did not fully understand and asked when she would be coming back. He explained that only good people go there, that they are so happy there, that it would be selfish of us to want them back and that one day we would all be there together. I began to cry and he took me back to my father, who gathered me in his arms and we three returned home.

In later years, my father told me how my mother had known she was dying and before the end came, she told him that God was calling her and that she would like him to let her go freely according to God's will. Her last wish was for her children as she said "Above all, take good care of the children. Put them first, we must not think of ourselves."

My mother was a woman of deep faith which had a lasting influence on all the family. I barely remember her but I have a very happy and strong recollection of going to the Church with her. I loved the singing and the smell of incense from the altar at Benediction and when she would look down approvingly at us, sometimes I would catch her eye and that eternal smile of hers and would sing for all I was worth.

She used to sing a little Northern lullaby which haunts me yet. It is the story of a young mother who lost her baby boy to the fairies and how that mother found her boy again in Paradise.

My mother's death on the 27th February 1927 at the age of 34, heralded many changes in our way of life. For my father, the good days were over and for Charlie, his troubles were beginning.

Wedding Photograph: Joseph Donnelly and Rose McCaughey, 1913.

CHAPTER TWO

"Youth's lonely, austere joy . . ."

Charlie was only twelve years old when my mother died. My father had eight children to look after, the youngest of them only a few weeks old. We moved to our new home "Moorland" where we were to live for the next eighteen months or so.

The fields and the surrounding countryside gave us a great sense of freedom and despite the loss of my mother, I have only happy memories of these days. But for my father, they were difficult times. A close friend and neighbour of ours remarked to me some years later in reference to my father's life in Dundalk, that it had seemed to her that everything he put his hands to turned to gold but now, in "Moorland", the opposite would be nearer the truth.

He had to spend more time looking after the family at home, although Charlie and Tom did their best to help after school. He was forced to leave the running of the shop in the hands of others with resulting loss of profits; his cattle trading also suffered. Neighbours and friends let him know how wild his children were becoming and that he ought to do something about it. Some were inferring that he should re-marry; my mother's sister, Sr. Carmel, a Holy Faith nun, even threatened to leave the convent to look after the children. The idea of re-marriage did not appeal to him and he struggled on as best he could.

His two sisters, Lizzie and Minnie, who had moved on to Dublin where they had acquired some property, offered to help. They took it in turns to visit Dundalk for a few weeks at a time. My aunts were genuinely concerned for our welfare in every respect but particularly our spiritual welfare. They made sure we always had our rosary beads in our pockets! They devoted their lives to the creation of bursaries for the education of young priests for the missions. They had wills of iron and a very strong faith, but, intellectually, they were the end product of the paternalism of the Church in those days.

They appreciated my father's business acumen and never failed to consult him in all such matters. He, on the other hand, considered the rearing of young children to be the natural domain of women and was happy to leave the family in their care. But their authoritarian and rigid approach to discipline, together with their pre-occupation with our immortal souls only succeeded in injuring the bond of trust that existed in the family.

Around this time Charlie began to show an interest in reading and writing. My aunts were worried about his choice of books, as anything other than the lives of the saints or Catholic Truth Society pamphlets were highly suspect. As it happened, St. Francis of Assissi was Charlie's favourite saint but where my aunts would pray to him, Charlie would also see the need to follow him. Charlie acquired books wherever he could but I fear they were read under a blanket at night.

His writing efforts were in the form of short stories which he sent to 'Our Boys', the Christian Brothers' magazine. I remember a big fuss over a story he wrote about the Civil War. It was rejected because it was considered to be too controversial. Thirty years later, the incident was remembered by one of the staff of 'Our Boys'. Some of these stories survive.

Poetry also interested him and what must have been one of his earliest poems caused a furore with my aunts. They found a poem he had written about a local girl, Maureen Treanor, a pretty redhead, and confronted Charlie with it, forbidding him any further contact with the girl. The poem hasn't survived but Maureen appears in a short story which he wrote later in Dublin . . .

> "The idea of a female saviour who would rescue him from bitterness was frequently in his mind. Every evening setting out, he hoped that before returning he would have been caressed by a girl. Sometimes he would reproach himself that he was being false to Maureen, and would resolve as he walked: I swear I will think of no-one but Maureen for the next half hour."

Up to this time, my father was not aware of any problem with Charlie. In fact, he had every reason to be proud of him and had great hopes for his future. Neither had he any cause for concern about the rest of us, for despite our wildness, the important thing to him was that we were united and happy. However, under my aunts' influence, he began to have some doubts about the situation, and about Charlie in particular.

My aunts were becoming tired of all the travelling to and from Dundalk, (they had already taken my younger sister, Carmel, to Dublin to live with them), and they suggested that he sell his interests, lock, stock and barrel, and move to Dublin where they could keep their eyes on us without neglecting their own business. He resisted the idea for some time but the final straw came for him when, on returning from a fair in the north where he had purchased some cattle, he found that he had lost a couple of the animals. It was a cold winter's day. He retraced his steps and located the animals in a dealer's yard in Newry into which they had strayed with another herd. After much argument with the dealer, he recovered the cattle and began the return journey to Dundalk. The combination of cold, rain and tiredness, convinced him that there must be an easier way of earning a living and so, he finally decided to move to Dublin.

My father often regretted this decision as it involved uprooting the family from an area they had grown used to and initiated a whole new set of problems, mainly centering around Charlie. His friends and neighbours in Dundalk had tried to pursuade him to stay in the town and the parish priest also tried to intervene but consideration of what was best for the family in general was the deciding factor.

So, in the spring of 1929, the family moved to Dublin. At first we were unable to move into the house at Mountjoy Square which my father had bought, as there were some repairs to be completed. In the meantime, we stayed at our aunts' house at Eccles Street for a few weeks. Having been used to the freedom of the countryside around Moorland, we felt very restricted and the conduct of my younger brothers and myself became a cause for concern to my aunts. My father then decided that we should move to Mountjoy Square whether the repairs were completed or not.

We soon settled down to a regular pattern of life, part of which was a weekly visit to Eccles Street to my Aunts' house where we were expected to perform our party pieces. Unlike it had been in Dundalk, we were now performing because it was expected, and, as time went on, we were less inclined to do so. Our party pieces over and the rosary recited, we would return home.

Arrangements had been made for our schooling. Charlie and my brother, Tom, were to go to the Christian Brothers' school, O'Connell's, North Richmond Street, to complete their secondary education and the remainder of the family was sent to local primary schools.

Unknown to my father, Charlie never registered at O'Connell's. Instead, he set out on a course of self-education and spent most of his time in libraries reading and writing or wandering around the streets of Dublin. A short story from this period details these wanderings:

> "In the evenings he used to walk along through the streets: Eccles Street and Upper Gardiner Street and Mountjoy Square and Gardiner's Row and Frederick Street. The placid Georgian houses in the dusk and the small treelined park in which tennis was played, evoked in his mind a faint superposition on themselves of drawing rooms and stately women, carriages and horses' trappings and aristocratic men."

Tom, however, attended school as arranged and made efforts to cover up for Charlie. But eventually, after the first term, when fees became due, my father discovered the truth. Charlie's extraordinary course of action was consistent with his rate of development and maturity which had accelerated since my mother's death, resulting in a growing self-reliance and independence. Also unknown to my father, Charlie had been developing in other directions. We lived within a stone's throw of the Dublin slums and here Charlie witnessed poverty on a scale he had never seen before.

This awakened in him a thirst for justice. The observation he had made as a very young boy on a fair day in Dundalk was maturing and led him to question the structures of society, religious and political, into which he had been born.

He discovered the Workers' College at 63 Eccles Street where he met people like Peadar O'Donnell and his wife, Lil, who were seeking radical solutions to the injustices around them. He began to read their publications and propaganda and to attend lectures which were mainly on the history of the Labour Movement and Trade Unionism, given by Peadar O'Donnell and Brian O'Neill, among others.

Peadar O'Donnell and the groups he directed, namely the militant Republican I.R.A., Saor Eire and the Revoluntionary Workers' Group, had Socialist leanings. The reaction of both Church and State to these groups was to denounce them as communistic, 'enemies of religion' and a threat to the State. In fact, very few members of these groups were communists.

My father was very concerned at the direction Charlie's life was taking. There were frequent arguments between Charlie and my father, assisted by my aunts, and they made their position quite clear. It was not for them to question the structures, religious and political, but especially the stewardship of the Lord's anointed, and unless Charlie was prepared to find his proper place in society, he would be in serious trouble. Charlie, though only fifteen years of age, stood by his views. His free intellect and spirit would not be imprisoned by middle-class standards.

My father was not satisfied to leave matters at that and decided to seek the help of a good priest, a Jesuit, whom he respected. Charlie had a long talk with this priest who found nothing wrong with his Christianity but he did advise him that as his father and aunts only had his welfare at heart, it was not right for him to worry them by discussing such matters with them as they could not possibly understand his point of view. On the other hand, he let my father know that he need have no fear regarding Charlie's faith. If anything, he was inclined to take his Christianity too seriously and, as regards his politics, it was probably a phase he was going through and time would take care of both. The net result of this interview was that their fears for his spiritual welfare were somewhat allayed.

However, Charlie's ideas regarding religion were disturbing to my father. He was deeply critical of a religion that seemed, in those days, irrelevant to matters of justice.

On one occasion, Charlie had asked in confession how one was meant to interpret Christ's injunction to give away one's coat, and he was not satisfied with the answer that it should not be taken too literally.

There still remained the problem of Charlie's schooling and, as the old arguments resurfaced, my father, in consultation with my aunts, decided that if Charlie was not prepared to go to school in the normal way, he would have to go to work.

In desperation, my aunts consulted a Mr. Walshe, a tenant of theirs, who was a cabinet maker and rented the mews at the rere of their house in Eccles Street. Although Mr. Walshe and my aunts were opposite in character and lifestyle, they had become very friendly over a period of time. They regarded him as a good tradesman and a man of the world. He was very respectful towards them and very helpful when it came to doing repairs around the house. Charlie was later to describe the relationship between them in a short story as follows —

> I'd better not be keeping you from your work, Mr. Walshe, I see you're busy. We wanted to talk to you for a minute but it can wait till some other time.
> Well, that it can't, Miss Donnelly. Ladies first, that's what I always try to put into the head of this rascal here. I'll go inside now Miss Donnelly. Joe, leave that be and start on the other two . . . Use your own plane.
> He followed Miss Donnelly, bending to pass through the low doorway and taking off his apron which he threw on top of some sheets of plywood beside the door.
> The elder Miss Donnelly was pouring tea. Three cups were set. She greeted Mr. Walshe with the extreme pleasure which both these ladies always showed on seeing him. Mr. Walshe sat down. He seemed curiously out of place, self-conscous, sitting at a table. Ten years he had been estranged from his wife, without communication with his two children, absorbed in his work, surrounded by a wall of falsehood. Towards the two Miss Donnellys with their quiet routine lives, he had contracted an extraordinary affection. To them he was the paragon among men, a paragon of wisdom and virtue. The insidious stories told of him left them completely unaffected. They clung to their belief in him and he, with all the strength of his wasted lonely life, clung to their

affection and esteem. Repeated offers of more suitable and cheaper workshops came to him, but he let them go, stopping on in the dark little loft with its difficult entry and inconvenient position . . .

Strange as it may seem, there was great understanding between them. Of course, knowing my Aunt Lizzie, she must have seen a possible convert here. Mr. Walshe, on the other hand, always knew whom he was talking to and if he had the right listener there was no place he had not seen or nothing he could not do.

My aunts found him more than willing to help on this occasion and he greatly appreciated their confidence in him. However, he would have to meet 'this problem' before he would commit himself.

Consequently, on one of Charlie's visits to Eccles Street, my aunts arranged a little chat at which this man was present. Formalities and trivialities attended to, the conversation was steered towards justice and the structure of society. My aunts explained their position regarding the underprivileged, expressing sympathy for their plight, but they considered that the poor were best served by charitable organisations such as the St. Vincent de Paul Society. Charlie, for his part, realised that the poor needed charity but, above all, they needed justice as they were the victims of a privileged society and if this structure was the product of *our* Christianity, then there must be something wrong with it.

During this dialogue, the man who knew everything, said nothing. He knew that in a little while Charlie would be gone. He would then have another cup of tea and another cigarette and command the stage.

His opinion of Charlie was that he was indeed a remarkable boy but that he had too much spirit. Also 'a little learning was a dangerous thing', and this boy had an overdose of it and the cure was — hard work. He proposed taking Charlie on as an apprentice and told my aunts that within six months, he would guarantee that Charlie would be as normal as anyone else. Indeed, in his opinion, the more education Charlie got, the more he would want to change society and he saw no future in that. He would be better using his hands rather than his head.

My aunts brought this suggestion to my father, who reluctantly agreed as he could see no other course at the time. He knew it was far short of what he had hoped for Charlie and that he was capable of more.

This was the start of long and toilsome days for Charlie. However, he took it in his stride. My father bought him a new kit of tools and I can remember watching him do some homework. He took a board and put it across a chair. He then drew a line and proceeded to saw. As I watched I noticed the sawdust gather on the line, so I went over and blew it off. Charlie said, "That's right, Joe, you can't saw straight unless you can see the line." This was not enough for me and I remained there staring. He understood and so, for the first time, I held a saw in my hand and completed the cut.

Contrary to the expectations of Mr. Walshe and my aunts, Charlie's self-education continued and in the workshop he was quick to recognise in the veneering of cheap timber a fair reflection of our society.

In his spare time, he wrote poetry and prose, mainly short stories, and was developing his musical tastes, the plaintive traditional Gaelic airs having a particular appeal for him. His favourite singer at the time was Count John McCormack. His earliest surviving poem was written in tribute to the singer and dates from this period.

The house in Mountjoy Square was very large and so my father decided to rent out some of the rooms to tenants.

Our first tenant was a man named ffrench-Mullen, an interesting man who became very friendly with the family. He was a Republican and was intellectually inclined. He would come down to our kitchen every other night and his arrival would always coincide with the end of our night prayers and rosary. I could see that my father and Charlie enjoyed listening to him. He was of a very intense disposition and I honestly believe I never saw him sit down. My brothers and I always had our baths on Saturday nights and I remember one Saturday in particular, as we were roasting ourselves in front of the fire after our wash, ffrench-Mullen was relating an experience he had had while a Republican prisoner in England. A musician, he had been given permission to play the organ at Mass on a particular Sunday, at the end of which he played The Soldier's Song and all the prisoners stood to attention while the guards looked on in consternation. Apart from this story, I could never understand anything he had to say, for he was far too complicated for me. I was only eight years old at the time. But my eye was always on him and a thought once struck me as I watched him walking up and down that kitchen floor, talk, talk, talk, — "If this man doesn't stop visiting us, he will surely make a track on our floor."

Our second tenant was a lady, Maria Farrelly, a dress designer. My father explained to my brothers and myself that our behaviour would have to improve and this little game of ours of running upstairs and sliding down the bannisters would have to cease. My father didn't have to worry about Mr. ffrench-Mullen as he didn't seem to mind the noise and why would he, when he was making his own. He was fond of music and played the violin!

The day Miss Farrelly arrived, Charlie helped her settle in and hung curtains for her. That evening at tea-time, Miss Farrelly was the main topic of conversation and Charlie said she was a very kind lady and explained that she had offered him a half-crown for his trouble, which of course, he hadn't wanted to accept but rather than offend her, he had agreed to take it. On hearing this, I let him know that if Miss Farrelly wanted someone to run errands for her, then I was her man! This remark was followed by silence and a look from my father. He said nothing, he didn't have to, that look was enough.

As it happened, I was to run many an errand for this lady as she soon became my step-mother. My father's second marriage took place in October, 1930. My step-mother was kind to us and we always felt free in her company. Her coming brought some changes in the family. My aunts' influence was not as strongly felt and Charlie was to get a new deal. She felt strongly that Charlie was wasting his time learning a trade and should be sent to University. Accordingly, much to the regret of Mr. Walshe, Charlie was taken out of apprenticeship and sent to a private school to begin an intensive course of studies in preparation for his entry into University. In the space of six months, he covered the course and took his matriculation. He entered University College, Dublin in October 1931 at the age of seventeen.

My father's second marriage was not a complete success as my step-mother had different aspirations. She wanted to continue with her career and socialise while he had hoped she would devote more time to the children and live a quiet family life. Eventually, they were to establish a civilised, tolerant attitude towards each other although they pursued their separate interests. They had one child, Philip, who died of menengitis when he was two and a half years old.

CHAPTER THREE

> "Are the moods voiceless? For I have no words.
> Blood cannot talk, although it cracks the skin."

Charlie entered U.C.D. as an Arts student, his subjects being Logic, English, History and Irish. He was now in his element and in the early thirties the college was a lively, vibrant place bursting with a wealth of young talent. Some of his contemporaries were, Brian O'Nuallain, Liam Redmond, Cearbhall O'Dalaigh, Denis Devlin, Mary Lavin, Cyril Cusack, Brian Coffey, Mervyn Wall, Niall Montgomery, Donagh MacDonagh and Niall Sheridan, all acquaintances, but some became close friends.

I recall talking to Charlie about his new-found friends as, when he first entered college, I shared a room with him. The three he spoke of most were Donagh MacDonagh, Niall Sherian and Niall Montgomery. Sheridan was editor of the college magazine, Comhthrom Feinne, and as Charlie said, was mad about literature. Of Montgomery, Charlie remarked — "He will be important one day". Montgomery, an architectural student, was the son of the then Film Censor. MacDonagh, son of the executed 1916 leader Thomas MacDonagh seemed to be his closest friend.

He enjoyed the exchange of ideas among people of his own age and used all the facilities open to him for reading, writing and sharing his political views. He lost no time in submitting articles and poetry to the college magazine, through which he met Sheridan, who recalls the meeting as follows:

> I first saw his name when he contributed a story to the College Magazine. There was a vigour and freshness about that story which made me anxious to know Donnelly. Shortly afterwards, when I began to edit the magazine, I wrote to him for further work and arranged to meet him in the Main Hall of the College, then the only available rendezvous for students. I remember that meeting clearly because it had a touch of anti-climax. I had somehow got the idea that Donnelly would be a tall, fair-haired and athletic medical student. It was a bad guess. He turned out to be less than average height, diffident in manner, with a lean earnest face and blue eyes of extraordinary clarity. He looked absurdly young. During the next few years I saw a great deal of him, and I retain a vivid memory of that spare figure, walking with a slight spring in his steps, the fine head carried high, a book or two tucked securely under his arm.

He contributed articles on a variety of subjects including literature, modern philosophy and politics. His literary interests were wide-ranging. MacDonagh and Sheridan remember that his particular enthusiasms were Keats, Shelley and the Romantics, although he also knew Eliot, Joyce, the Elizabethans, Kafka, Hopkins, the journal of Barbellion and many French poets in translation, especially Rimbaud and Baudelaire. Sheridan recalls:

> When I first knew Donnelly he was reading Shelley, exploring literature for himself. At this period he read eagerly and extensively, discovering with particular delight the letters of Keats and the Journal of Barbellion. He was attracted by the intellectual rather than the sensuous element in literature — a typical instance was his almost chronic preoccupation with Keats' phrase about "the earnest stars". It thrilled him in its manifestation of fine sensibility and unique complexity of thought.

At home my father was sorting out his affairs to advantage and had purchased two new properties, one of which was number 3 North Great George's Street. My step-mother wanted to live in North Great George's Street and on moving in, we found our next door neighbour to be James Dillon, T.D. Many a ball crossed over the garden wall never to return. On reflection, I can sympathise with Mr. Dillon but at the time, as children, we were aggrieved.

In these days, nothing was too good for Charlie. He was to have his own room where he could entertain his friends whenever he wished. The room was re-decorated to his own taste and the old pictures came down and up went some sketches (a gift from his friend, Niall Montgomery) together with prints of old Dublin. Of course, I had to move out!

Charlie enjoyed student life and attended the usual round of social events and parties. In an article in University Review in the early fifties, MacDonagh remembers:

> We gave a party at which many pints were lowered and many bad jokes and puns were made ... while Donnelly sat on the floor with his back to the wall murmuring disgustedly Keat's phrase: "Why did I laugh tonight?" He and Denis Devlin, then a Surrealist poet, agreed that they were the only important and serious people present — as indeed they were. Afterwards eight of our guests climbed into Pierce Fitzgerald's Baby Austin to go home. Donnelly all the time imploring Pierce to drive carefully. 'You have a car-load of geniuses aboard,' he said, 'Irish literature depends on your brakes.!'

MacDonagh's assent to the remark that Charlie was indeed one of the few important people at that party was no mere throwaway comment.

Sheridan had said that 'he had quite the most mature mind I have ever come across.' His reputation as a poet spread through the college and he became something of a celebrity. Cyril Cusack remembers that he was known as 'the young Shelley'.
Regardless of the admiration of his friends and his ability to speak out on matters he believed in, he was also very shy socially, but particularly about his poetry. According to Sheridan:

> There was a considerable contrast between Don (MacDonagh) and Charlie in the way they presented their new works. If Don had a new poem in his pocket he'd stop you in the street and hit you over the head with it. He'd chain you to the railings until you heard it all out. Charlie would very, very tentatively, almost accidentally produce it and one would have to work on him to get him to read it.

He was also something of a controversial figure as his political views became known. He spoke out against the rise of Fascism in Europe and the political structures at home. His main opposition came from the Christian Front element in the University, some of whom saw the rise of Fascism as a healthy phenomenon. The following satirical notice which appeared in Comhthrom Feinne in April, 1932 speaks for itself.

To the eternal memory
of
Charles Donnelly
"The Apostle of Freedom"
Garrotted by the long-suffering
Capitalistic University College
Dublin
in the year of the revolution
142
****

"The Sun is shining brightly on the lonely grave, a
luxuriant bed of nettles, where Donnelly is laid."
****

Erected by his loving comrades: Joyce, Trotsky, Lenin,
General Ina and the OGPU, Moscow.
****

"He's gone to join Voltaire and Rousseau in the Land of
Eternal Warmth."

Brian O'Neill, late of the Irish Press, recalls meeting Charlie at a meeting of the University Marxist Society in U.C.D. The Society also met at Trinity College but had little success at U.C.D. as the College authorities were suspicious of anything of a left-wing nature in those days.

Charlie's increasing literary interests, combined with his political activities, interfered with his studies and his attendance at lectures became infrequent. He failed his first year examinations and was cautioned by his teachers.

His political beliefs gradually began to take precedence over his studies, particularly following his joining the Republican Congress. His passion for social justice found expression in his commitment to the struggle of the working classes. His commitment was total and his private rebellion was now public.

The previous year 1932 had been a time of great political uneasiness. The Republicans, having been frustrated in the Civil War, realised that power could only come through the ballot box. In the election of 1932, Fianna Fail under the leadership of DeValera, meant business. It was a time when those who had nothing, had hope and those who had something, said their prayers. I can remember a maid of ours named Lizzie, whose eyes would light up at the mention of DeValera's name. To her and to many others, DeValera had the answer to everything. This was the time of 'the great illusion', we were back on the road to the Republic.

However, to my father, Republicanism was synonymous with Socialism as it was to some Republicans and for their benefit, DeValera had no difficulty in equating his position with that of Connolly in regard to social justice. In our home, many a rosary was said that he would not make it.

In any event, the issue was black and white, Dev. or Cosgrave. Feelings ran high on both sides and there was little room for reason. Cosgrave's meetings were protected by the A.C.A. (Army Comrades Association) while DeValera's had the full backing of the I.R.A. DeValera won the day but to Charlie, in spite of the change to Fianna Fail, he saw the old structure emerge as before with a new coat of paint, a new shade of green.

Charlie, having failed his first year examinations, was obliged to repeat first year. In the summer of 1933 he passed first Arts with honours in English and Logic. His activities in the Republican Congress continued. Its founder members were Peadar O'Donnell, George Gilmore, Frank Ryan and Michael Price, and its foundation brought about a split in the I.R.A. Those on the right were interested in armaments not ideologies and were prisoners of the Church and the past.

Charlie found within the Congress, all the scope and freedom he needed. He first came to the notice of the leadership through an article he had written under a nom-de-plume for Reynolds News which dealt with the Republican Congress. Peadar O'Donnell was particularly impressed and was later to remark — 'I knew I had found something'.

His rise in the Republican Congress was swift and following the first full meeting of the Congress in September, 1934, he was elected a member of the national executive.

Earlier that year in the Spring, he had founded an anti-fascist group called the Student Vanguard. He tried to convert his University friends to his way of thinking but without success. He once succeeded in getting Donagh MacDonagh to chair one of the meetings of the Student Vanguard. MacDonagh was to write later:

> I had never been chairman anywhere and when it was discovered that there were Blueshirts present in the hall, trouble seemed inevitable ... The trouble started fairly soon and private fights of many kinds developed quickly all over the hall. I banged on the table but nobody took much notice, in fact the noise increased considerably. Then Donnelly jumped up on the table and shouted for order, which he astonishingly got. After that he took control of everything, including the chair and even managed to get the Blueshirts a safe conduct out of the building. They put up their knuckledusters and under the protection of Frank Ryan slipped down the stairs and away. From that on it was Donnelly's meeting. He put motions, passed resolutions and read the manifesto which he had written. Next day the papers carried the story 'College students in scene'. 'Blueshirts in scuffle in Dublin Hall!' Donnelly was delighted, but my connection with the Student Vanguard was at an end.

The movement was to peter out despite the fact that there was quite a good proportion of liberal minded students in the University but protest at a safe distance and revolution as an intellectual exercise were not enough for Charlie. As Cyril Cusack remarked later — 'We went part of the way, but he went all the way.'

My father was becoming concerned about Charlie's lack of progress in his studies and voiced his concern about Charlie's friends and opinions to Donagh MacDonagh on one of MacDonagh's visits to our home. In trying to ascertain where this apparently well-mannered though lively young student stood politically, my father was left more concerned than ever when MacDonagh stood up boldly and stated 'You can trust me in anything except the Republic.'

When he told this incident to my step-mother, she told him of her encounter with another of Charlie's friends who had called to the house. She had made tea for this young man whom she decribed as having a 'good clean look about him'. Her conversation on general topics had left her with no cause for concern, her remark to my father being — 'if they are all like this young man, you have nothing to worry about.'

During this time, Charlie met and fell in love with Cora Hughes, a close friend of Donagh MacDonagh's sister Barbara (Redmond). She was slim and attractive with refined features and light red hair, as had his first love, Maureen, in Dundalk. She was a member of Cumann na mBan and came from a Republican background, her father being a close friend of DeValera. Cora's father had been best man at DeValera's wedding and DeValera was later to become Cora's godfather.

Cora, who had an M.A. in Celtic Studies, had strong political leanings of a radical nature. She was a very concerned person. An obituary points out, "When Cora came into public life, she found the Republic was not enough. The task of freeing Irish humanity from economic bondage took on the aspect of a faith, a religion. She could have had all the comfort in life she wanted but Cora could not eat while others hungered, sleep while others were homeless, be inactive while others were oppressed."

She and Charlie had much in common, similar views, similar goals, similar middle-class backgrounds. In addition, they were both experiencing opposition in their homes because of their political involvement, both eventually choosing to leave their respective homes. But the most significant element drawing them together was the depth of their commitment to their shared cause, which would demand the ultimate from them both by different means.

She had many admirers, including George Gilmore with whom she had had a relationship prior to meeting Charlie. Gilmore was to relate in an unpublished novel, 'The Gold Flag', the encroachment of this younger man into the relationship. However, he insists there was never any bitterness:

> The three of us were always good friends and good comrades. With people like Charlie and Cora there would never be any question of small-mindedness or jealousy. I believe that Charlie loved Cora and that she returned that love — but it had a purity, almost a spiritual intensity to it, although it wasn't platonic, which meant that there was no room for meanness of mind on anyone's part; least of all mine, because Charlie and I were closer than brothers. Even though he was younger, he was old

beyond his years, politically and emotionally very mature. I loved him almost as much as I loved Cora, which is more than a cynic like me would say is possible to love anyone.

My father welcomed the news of Charlie's relationship with Cora as he hoped it would have a stabilising influence on him. He was prepared to do everything he could to encourage the young couple, even down to purchasing a house for them if they were planning to marry.

I can remember her calling to our home one evening. I opened the door and she asked to see Charlie, saying she was his girl-friend. I was struck by her fine appearance. I showed her to the drawingroom and called Charlie. While she was waiting, my father came to greet her. In the ensuing conversation, he told her how he felt about Charlie's activities and was greatly disappointed when he realised that Cora was as much committed to political activism as Charlie was. Indeed, she informed my father that she would stand behind Charlie in anything he did and would encourage his political interests. As far as my father was concerned, Cora was an additional cause for concern in Charlie's life. Likewise, Cora's family saw Charlie as another bad influence in her life and discouraged the relationship.

Nothing daunted, the young couple continued their involvement with each other and with the Republican Congress.

Charlie and Cora worked side by side leading workers' marches, speaking on platforms at street corners, rent and eviction battles, and picketing. Paddy Byrne, a Congress activist recalls:

> I can picture himself and Cora Hughes, having organised one of the most spectacular of demos I have ever taken part in, striding out under the risen banners of the papal encyclical and the tricolour, at the head of some thousand of the city's poor, a procession of women and kids and perambulators, to the house of the Lord Mayor. It was a people's challenge on a big scale.

The offensive of the Congress on the Dublin slums met with strong opposition from Church and State. A report in the Irish Times at the time reads:

> The Roman Catholic Hierarchy has warned its flock very urgently against the menace of Communism but the warning must be futile so long as 4,830 tenement houses shelter 25,320 families in the heart of Dublin. It is almost a miracle that hitherto Communism has not flourished aggressively in that hideous soil.

Congress activists were frequently harassed by the police. Charlie was a popular target. An old family friend remembers an occasion on the corner of Cathal Brugha Street and O'Connell Street when Cora and Charlie were speaking. A group of policemen were overheard by this friend discussing whether to wait until the end of the meeting to arrest him. She promptly warned Charlie who left the meeting unnoticed.

Apart from street activities, Charlie was a regular contributor to the Congress newspaper.

Within the membership of the Congress, Charlie was not entirely accepted. Some members were suspicious of him mainly because of his middle-class background and his youth. Again Paddy Byrne remembers:

> My first impression, that of a subdued, semi-hostile bossy little person, neither typical undergrad not typical worker. He came from a middle-class environment. But he had shrewdness like our own in diplomacy and fantastic naïvete in other matters . . . we nevertheless did not take him 'into the family circle', so to speak. His individualism was a bit too high for us.

But later on, following the Rathmines Congress, when Charlie voted with O'Donnell, Gilmore and Ryan, for the 'Minority Resolution', Byrne says he was accepted right away and that he, personally, never experienced any uneasiness about meetings he was asked to chair if Charlie's name was on the poster as speaker. But George Gilmore believed that Charlie was often hurt by his comrades' attitudes but he, nevertheless, excused their suspicions.

By the summer of 1934, Charlie had abandoned his studies and as a result of his political activities, found himself imprisoned for two weeks in July 1934 on charges arising out of a picket on a clothing factory, where workers were attempting to form a union and were striking for the right to do so.

While he was serving his sentence, my step-brother, Philip, died and Charlie was released for the funeral.

It is not possible for me to describe adequately the effect these events had on my father. He was basically a gentle and simple man, though formidable in business, with an innate decency and integrity. Most of all, he had a hatred of violence. His main interest in life was the welfare of his family and he was seriously concerned about the effects of Charlie's activities on the family. A conventional Catholic, my father was influenced by the hysterical attitude of the Church towards

Socialism, 'the Red cancer', and our pulpits were preoccupied with its eradication. In comparing his position with that of the Dillon family next door, he remarked: "Politics were a blessing for the Dillons but a curse for us."

Charlie remained as committed as ever to his political beliefs and once again was arrested on the 14th September 1934 for picketing the Bridewell in Dublin where some Congress activists were being held. He was fined and refused to pay, but the fine was paid on his behalf, probably by my father.

My father saw all this as the disintegration of his hopes and as far as he could see, Charlie was throwing his future to the wind. He tried, in his level-headed way to convince Charlie that before he could help others, he must first put himself in a position where it would be possible for him to do something positive. Otherwise, far from founding a new society, he would find an early grave. As my father searched for answers, all he found was his own crucifixion.

Charlie tried to explain that he knew exactly what he was doing and was not concerned for his own material welfare. He knew there was no seat in the structure he could not have if he wished to pursue the like but he viewed the structure as an unjust one, designed by the fox, for the fox, and only the fox would thrive in it. It had little in keeping with the spirit of the Proclamation and much less with the teachings of Christ. Indeed, Charlie's view of Christianity was that the social teachings of the gospel were far more radical than Marxism and, according to George Gilmore, he always retained that view.

There could be no compromise in the respective positions of father and son and, as was so well described in MacDonagh' poem, written after Charlie's death, he would be a 'a willing sacrifice on the altar of his integrity.'

The situation became intolerable for my father and he asked Charlie to make a choice between his home and a return to his studies or his political involvement. At the same time, my father was hoping against hope that, in his own words, 'Charlie would come to his senses.' However, Charlie chose to leave home.

He was now facing a period of great hardship. His friends recall that he was sleeping rough on park benches or on the floors of friends' lodgings whenever he could. My brother, Tom, always loyal and ready to support Charlie, often smuggled him into the mews at the rere of the house. Despite his personal difficulties he continued with his political activities.

His relationship with Cora continued to be a source of consolation to him at this time. He was also helped by Mrs. Owen Dudley-Edwards who took him into her home in Clontarf when she heard of his plight. Another place of welcome for him at this time was the Holy Faith Convent, Clarendon Street, Dublin, where he used to visit my mother's sister, Sr. Mary Carmel. She never questioned his motives and later described him as being 'more spirit than flesh.'

Early in 1935, he was once again arrested with Cora and several others for picketing a shop. On the 12th January, he was charged with assembly so as to cause obstruction, besetting a shop and threatening behaviour. He was sentenced to a month in prison or fines totalling £5.10s. This time the fines were not paid and he was duly imprisoned.

Cora was also imprisoned despite appeals from her father to his old Blackrock College friend, DeValera. Charlie makes reference to her trial in his poem 'The Flowering Bars' —

> After sharp words from the fine mind,
> protest in court,
> The intimate high head constrained . . .

While in prison, he had time to think about his position. He was finding it increasingly difficult to survive financially and his rough living was beginning to affect his health. Immediately following his release and much to the disappointment of Cora and his friends he decided to leave the country and go to London. He was now twenty years old.

CHAPTER FOUR

"Between rebellion as a private study and the public
Defiance, is simple action only in which will flickers
catlike, for spring."

On arrival in London, Charlie went straight to the Kilburn flat of his friend from Dublin, Leslie Daiken. Daiken, having graduated from Trinity College, had gone to London about a year earlier to find work. He had first met Charlie through Niall Sheridan who, as Daiken described later, 'had paraded his U.C.D. find in my rooms at Trinity with the air of an "Exhibit A".'

Daiken remembers the unexpected, early morning ringing of his doorbell. He welcomed Charlie and noted, with surprise, that he was now thinner and paler than he had been when he knew him in Dublin. However, he didn't ask or expect any explanation as to the 'why' of his coming but later on over a cup of coffee, Charlie volunteered an explanation —

"I just had to get out of that bloody place. It's hard to stand the stupidity any longer".

Without discussing the reasons behind this statement, Daiken could see the despair and heartache in his words. The previous six or seven months in Dublin had taken their toll. Apart from the difficulties of keeping body and soul together, he had been experiencing opposition from some rank and file members of the Republican Congress who were suspicious of him because of his middle-class background and his youth, but what had caused him most pain had been the separation from his home and family. He confided to Daiken that he had not really wanted to leave his home.

Now in London, he explained 'Burning his boats' meant farewells to his personal affections for men like George Gilmore and Frank Ryan and also for 'a certain woman.' The woman, of course, was Cora, with whom Daiken maintains Charlie was 'overwhelmingly in love'. His departure for London seemed to have created a strain in their relationship although they remained in touch and Cora visited him later on.

Finding a job was his first concern. Daiken introduced him around but remembers that he was more successful in winning friends than jobs — he had 'a gentle mannerly earnestness, a drawling inflection, where Dundalk had been overlaid by Dublin, even and toneless but musical, with lilt enough to intrigue the English ear.' In these early days he was forced into the usual round of low paid jobs, but optimism and the prospect of new outlets for his political activism lightened his life. Daiken recalls —

Those were heroic days of dream and struggle. We were each, one of the steam-hammers. A job was only a meal-ticket till the whole rotten system would crack up. To-morrow and to-morrow. We knew. Our household was crazy and Chekovian but entirely addicted to hope. Occupants of the other rooms were Sean Mulgrew, back from America with his calm Mayo dignity to whom Charlie was drawn till the very last goodbye, and his wife from a convent school in Germany; a 'spoilt priest' from a Hebrew Seminary; a Welsh miner and his wife; Alan McLarnon — a constant visitor. Charlie's presence in this queer menage acted as a catalyst. We all got on exceedingly well.

With Sean Mulgrew and Mick Kelly, an I.R.A. man from Ballinasloe who was later killed at Brunete during the Spanish Civil War, Charlie formed the first London branch of the Republican Congress and became its first chairman. He also co-operated with Daiken in producing Irish Front, the London journal of the Republican Congress. They co-edited twenty-three numbers of the journal, but Daiken admits many of the issues were written entirely by Charlie. His manifestoes, analyses and calls to action were largely effective in keeping the emigrant Irish in touch with their own and international political issues. To Dublin he sent articles on the situation in Britain for publication in the Congress newspaper which was edited by Frank Ryan.

The Labour Research Bureau commissioned him to prepare a survey on Irish Banking, which survives.

Irish Front was printed on a gestetner in the offices of the League Against Imperialism whose members invited him to speak on Irish matters on platforms all over the country. The League was a small united front organisation of the left with representatives from all over the British Empire and Colonies. Daiken says:

> There was nothing 'Tammany' or muscovite about his oratory; his style was unemotional and forceful; precise and extremely articulate. Once we were invited by the Magli Group (Indian students) to address them at Oxford. His address was magnificent, a memorable exegesis on the history of republican ideals.

Despite the demands of hard work by day and writing and editing at night, Charlie was relaxed and obviously enjoyed what he was doing. With his friends, he would sit and discuss literary and political topics over endless cups of tea or coffee. According to Daiken:

In poverty or plenty he always seemed preoccupied with thought, action, never his stomach or a bed. Class never entered into his respect for intellect, most immense of his enthusiasms. There was no casual adventure that excited him so much as having held conversation with a knowledgable person. 'A fine mind' was his favourite term of adoration. And if that mind happened to be a woman's, he would lean across the little cafe table, cigarette in his fingers like a tuning fork, till his elbow invaded the crockery and the toppling chair slipped. Afterwards: 'My God, you know, there's nothing as stimulating as a really intelligent woman.'

He confessed his loneliness for Cora and Daiken felt that although his life was full of action, it was empty of warmth. 'Talk was the hot-water bottle'. 'He talked the poetry and pathology of love better than any Proust.' Often short of money, he would prefer to buy a packet of good cigarettes and a book to having a scant meal.

His thoughts often turned to home and Daiken recalls playing some folkairs on the gramaphone in his room for Charlie and Ewart Milne, which had a deep affect on him. These were "Binori" sung by Richard Hayward as well as "An Leanbh Sidhe" and "The Coulin".

Through an English journalist friend, Montagu Slater, Charlie got a job in a newsagency in Fleet Street. This was more to his liking and he was earning more money. Slater was first struck on meeting Charlie by his 'political intelligence'. By this he didn't mean that he was just interested in politics, as by this time, 1935, according to Slater, most intelligent people and especially most young people, were awake to the political facts around them, "but to meet an advanced political brain in such a childlike exterior was a little like meeting a youthful chess prodigy. He had developed his natural detachment into a political outlook so nearly scientific and so little emotional that he was an uncommon figure in the London of 1935."

Slater also marvelled at Charlie's combined interest in poetry and literature together with politics, remarking: "The literary person in England, as a rule, is ignorant of political theory even when he is politically active; and the average political person is ignorant of contemporary poetry or literature. This young Irish poet-politician was exceptional enough to be interesting." They spent long hours in the discussion of such matters.

Charlie and Slater had a common enthusiasm for James Connolly and a desire to regain for him his rightful place in history as an international socialist leader. Slater urged Charlie to write a biography of Connolly which he began but never finished.

Slater recalls:

"Sometimes we used to argue about the Easter Rising and Donnelly would maintain, largely for the sake of argument, that its cost was greater than its achievement. Its highest cost was the life of Connolly himself and the Labour Movement in Ireland had paid heavily ever since for the absence of intellectual leadership."

In the meantime, my brother, Tom, on returning home from St. Patrick's College, Armagh for the Easter holidays, 1935, decided to give up his studies and follow Charlie to London. He acted out of concern for Charlie, feeling that he should be with him, and also out of consideration for my father who was anxious about Charlie. Tom hoped to be a link between them. He was always a peacemaker. On arrival in London, he stayed first in the already over-crowded flat at Kilburn. However, within a short time he had found a job in a factory in Acton where he also rented an apartment. He invited Charlie to live with him and they were to remain here for the duration of Charlie's stay in London.

Tom encouraged Charlie to write home and my father was very happy to hear from him. My father was particularly pleased to hear that Charlie was now working in Fleet Street and interpreted this news as an answer to prayer. At last, perhaps, Charlie was getting sense. But he knew nothing of Charlie's continued political activities and assumed that if Charlie now held a responsible position, he would have little time for politics.

One of the letters home was particularly welcome to me as it contained a warm invitation for me to go over for two or three weeks. My father was happy to let me go and I jumped at the opportunity. I was then thirteen years old. I was met at Euston by Tom who apologised for Charlie's absence saying that he was working late. I was to spend a fortnight in London where Charlie and Tom did their best to make my stay a happy one. I was with Charlie during the day and with Tom in the evenings, as one worked by day and the other by night. I have happy memories of being brought to see "Ruggles of Red Gap" which starred Roland Culver and Douglas Fairbanks, Jr., cups of coffee with nice pastries in cafes, visits to Grays Inn Road where Charlie was working on producing Irish Front, and a visit to a theatre to see a play concerning Easter Week which had been written by one of Charlie's friends. It was performed in the round and I can still remember the soldiers making their entrance through the auditorium.

Charlie always treated me as an adult and I tried to respond accordingly. On one occasion while walking down one of the main thoroughfares in London, I noticed a strike picket and remarked, 'I suppose they are looking for a just wage'. He looked at me with his friendly grin and asked, 'What is a just wage?'. I was a little taken aback and the best I could do was to suggest that the Pope would know all about that. He guessed immediately that I was referring to Pope Leo XIII's encyclical, *Rerum Novarum*, and remarked, 'Yes, Joe, but it is so watered down that all the good is gone out of it.'

I can also remember talking to him about the number of women in London who used make-up as it was not so much the fashion in Dublin at that time. His remark was — 'Don't you think it improves them.' I had to agree.

There were times when neither of them could be with me and, for these periods Tom bought a mini billiard table for my amusement. Once, during a game with Charlie, the table became a battlefield in the Russian Civil War and for the first time I heard the name Trotsky and of how he had created the Red Army out of a rabble and had finally broken all resistance to the revolutionary forces. This was my first introduction to Russian politics. I became very interested in Trotsky and on pursuing the subject further, I learnt from Charlie that Trotsky was then on the run, and the first important victim in a long line of purges. At a time when Moscow seemed to be providing answers for many of his contemporaries, Charlie was becoming suspicious of Stalin especially following the murder of Sergei Kirov in December 1934. (Kirov was a member of the central committee of the party and of the Politburo and also head of the party in Leningrad). This was an unpopular line of thought to some who were all too ready to label him a 'Trotskyite'. Tom remembers attending a meeting in London at which Charlie spoke. As shouts of 'Trotskyite' came from a number of hecklers in the hall, Tom quickly sprang to Charlie's defence, forgetting that Charlie was more than able to deal with the situation himself.

Politics seemed to form so much of the conversation between Charlie and Tom that I occasionally became involved. My ears pricked up once when I heard him talk about the balance of power and the inevitability of war. I asked him why and when and was it really inevitable. He explained that at that time the opposing forces were more or less balanced but if the balance of power shifted in Germany's favour, war would be inevitable because Fascism was a cancer which was growing and would not be stopped except by force. I was reminded of this later on when Hitler and Stalin signed the Non-Agression Pact of 1939. In his essay, "Fascism and the Humanist Outlook", Charlie wrote — "Fascism is the most finished statement of the philosophy of capitalism in decay."

On my return home I was sent to boarding school to the Marist Fathers in Dundalk with my twin brothers, Peter and Paul, leaving only my youngest brother, Anthony, at home as my two sisters were also away at school. The next time I was to see Charlie was when he paid a short visit home for Christmas 1935. It was to be the last time we would be together as a family. He invited my father to go to London, and my father agreed to go during the following summer.

Back in London, Charlie continued his busy round of activities. Leslie Daiken remembers 'life was one long continuum of "agit-prop", as was the fashionable term for it.' He contributed articles to left wing publications on a variety of subjects including history, politics, economics, banking, philosophy, as well as book reviews, short stories and poetry. He lectured to trade union groups on Irish History and Republicanism and became a member of a committee organised by the New Fabian Research Bureau, the purpose of which he explained in a letter to his friend in Dublin, Cecil ffrench Salkeld: "it was to draw up a statement of Britain's defence (sic) problems and a criticism from a technical point of view of the present war administration. Sounds queer work for me, but... necessary if the Labour Party is to make any progress at all."

As it happened his membership of this committee was not so strange, as he had been developing an interest in the theory of military strategy and had contributed a thesis on the tactics of the Spanish Peninsular Wars, for which he had been highly commended by Captain Basil Liddel Hart, the military historian, who was also a member of the committee. The Spanish Peninsular Wars were not those of the eighteenth century but referred to Nationaist uprisings in Asturias and Catalonia in 1934.

He was reading as much as ever and again Daiken recalls that he loved books and was never without one. He kept in touch with his friends in Dublin; George Gilmore remembered a letter in which Charlie spoke of his obsession with uniting politics and poetry, about reading Shelley in a political context and Connolly in a literary one. He was living life at a very fast pace.

In early summer 1936 my father went to London intending to stay for just a few days. Instead he was to spend a few weeks. Charlie spent a great deal of time with my father showing him the sights of London. He also brought him to see the intricacies involved in running the newsagency. Charlie's attentiveness and consideration gave my father a great deal of happiness. As Tom later remarked, he had never seen my father so happy and full of life. It was as though the years since my mother's death had been wiped away. Politics had faded into the background and neither had any wish to discuss them.

Tom had an ambition to start a confectionery business and my father wanted to help him in the venture. He was very pleased at this turn of events and immediately saw possibilities of a fresh start for the family as a whole in London. He discussed the pros and cons with Tom and promised to return to London later on to do something about it.

Shortly after his return to Dublin events which were to have a profound effect on the family and my father's plans and which would cost Charlie his life, broke loose.

In Spain, the Spanish Generals led by General Francisco Franco, rebelled against the Republican Government on the 17th of July 1936. The democratically elected, Popular Front Government according to Hugh Thomas's history of the Spanish Civil War, was composed of Liberal Republicans exclusively but depended on the working-class groups in the Cortes for its majority support. The democratically elected, Popular Front Government according to Hugh Thomas's history of the Spanish Civil War, was composed of Liberal Republicans exclusively but depended on the working-class groups in the Cortes for its majority support. Since the abdication of King Alfonso XIII in 1931, a struggle for power between Right and Left had been in progress. From 1931 to 1933, Spain was ruled by a coalition of Republicans and Socialists, but the reforms they introduced were considered too drastic for a people unused to democratic government. From 1933 to 1936, the Centre-Right Party took over power but was unable to reconcile the conflict that continued between the opposing forces of Left and Right. The result of the elections in February 1936 which brought the Popular Front to power was unacceptable to the traditional ruling class in Spain which consisted mainly of rich land owners, supported by the Church, and from which the office corps of the army was drawn. A coup was planned and its failure resulted in the out-break of the Civil War. out-break of the Civil War.

This war brought about an immediate division of Right and Left throughout the world. It captured the imagination of idealists of the Left and was to bring about a response in practical terms with the formation of the International Brigades consisting of volunteers from many countries, not least from Ireland.

However, in the absence of support through the non-intervention policies of the Western democracies, France, Britain and America, which was part of their appeasment policies towards Hitler, the Republican Government was forced to accept help from wherever it came. Stalin was able to manipulate this situation and the idealism of the Left and on the Right, the Spanish conflict provided a golden opportunity for Hitler, aided by Mussolini, to mount a 'dress rehearsal' for the inevitable world confrontation between Fascism and Democracy. But before this war would end, Stalin would have second thoughts about his involvement and would negotiate the non-agression pact with Hitler.

In London Charlie was preoccupied with the Civil War. He believed that intellectuals especially should take part in the struggle against Fascism, if only because they would be its first victims if it succeeded. He had been following the advance of Fascism in Europe up to this and saw the Spanish conflict as perhaps the last opportunity for democracy to make a stand.

He was an internationalist believing that true nationalism must have an international dimension and would quote Connolly to prove it. He held that Connolly and Casements' nationalism was essentially internationalist because it was anti-imperialist. He had always had difficulty in convincing his fellow Republican Congress members of this as they were more concerned with Irish issues and, as George Gilmore later admitted, failed to make the connection between Imperialism in Ireland and elsewhere.

With this in mind he began to write letters home to Frank Ryan and George Gilmore asking them to make a stand for the Spanish Republic on behalf of the Republican Congress. Congress was slow to respond to his request, having a variety of more immediate problems to deal with. Frank Ryan was of the opinion that they simply had not got the resources or the strength to take on the huge opposition to the Spanish Republic which had manifested itself in Ireland.

The Spanish Civil War was seen as a struggle between atheism and catholicism in this country and Church and State were behind Franco. Irish Catholic feeling was raised through reports of atrocities against priests and nuns and the burning of churches by the Republican forces and a sum of approximately £43,000 had been collected outside churches throughout Ireland to aid the forces of Franco.

On the 8th of September 1936, an editorial in the Irish Independent stated:

> On the one side is a so-called government which has abandoned all the functions of government to a Communist junta bent upon the destruction of personal liberty, the eradication of religion, the burning of churches, and the wholesale slaughter of the clergy. On the other side are the Patriot Army gladly risking liberty, property, and life, in the defence of their Faith — fighting the same fight that our Irish ancestors fought for centuries for the same cause.

Frank Ryan replied to Charlie and tried to explain the position at home but this didn't satisfy Charlie and he decided to come to Dublin in August in the hope of changing Ryan's attitude. At a meeting attended by Peadar O'Donnell, George Gilmore and Frank Ryan, a bitter row developed between Charlie and Frank Ryan in which Charlie accused Ryan of betraying the legacy of Connolly unless Congress publicly supported the Republican Government. Ryan's answer was that while Charlie had been writing accusing letters from London, he had been trying desperately to hold the rapidly weakening Congress together, at home and in America. The argument was finally settled and the meeting agreed that a message of support should be sent to the Spanish Republican Government. This was to set off a chain of events which would bring Ryan himself to Spain.

Charlie was pleased with the decision and spent some time in Dublin with family and friends. He had already made up his mind to go to Spain himself but did not tell the family of his plans. He saw Cora again and she and George Gilmore strongly discouraged him from going to Spain as did his college friends, but he would not be deterred. Niall Sheridan says:

> The Spanish Civil War was a very hot issue when we were young and, of course, we were all on the anti-Franco side. But he took it even more seriously. This was the showdown between Fascism and the rest. MacDonagh and myself were very saddened, but not surprised when he came and said he was going to fight against Franco. We spent a whole night trying to convince him that any fool could carry a rifle but that he could do a lot more important work by staying alive. In fact there are echoes of that night's argument in a very fine poem that Don wrote when we got the news of Charlie's death.

Before Charlie returned to London, there was reaction from the Church to the telegram of support that had been sent to the Spanish Government by Congress. On the 20th September in St. Peter's Church in Drogheda, Cardinal McRory publicly denounced the Republican Congress and suggested that the State should suppress such movements. Frank Ryan replied to the Cardinal on September 22nd stating that the message had merely been one of 'sympathy and support to the Spanish, Catalan and Basque peoples in their fight against Fascism'. He ended his reply as follows. — "Finally, may I assure your Eminence that, as a Catholic, 'I will take my religion from Rome', but that as an Irish Republican, I will take my politics neither from

Moscow nor Maynooth".' A further statement was issued by George Gilmore and Frank Ryan, as joint secretaries of the Republican Congress and was published in the Evening Mail, part of which said:

> We have no doubt that in Spain atrocities have been committed by both sides in the war. Needless to say we have no sympathy with such acts. Cardinal McRory has stated that he does not know much about the Republican Congress. There is no secret about our aims. The Republican Congress is a non-sectarian organisation of Irish men and women having as its aim the unity in action of the different Republican and working class organisations to achieve the unity and independence of Ireland.

General Eoin O'Duffy had been organising Irish Catholics to go to Spain to fight for Franco and many Irishmen on the left also wanted to volunteer.

Apparently, Peadar O'Donnell, George Gilmore and Frank Ryan were not very enthusiastic about this but an Irish unit of the left was formed in reply to what Frank Ryan called "Irish Fascism's intervention in the war against the Spanish Republic, namely, General O'Duffy's Volunteer force". It was expected that George Gilmore would lead the group but this proved impossible due to a leg injury he had sustained in a plane crash in Spain earlier that year while on a visit to the Basque region. Frank Ryan was the next obvious choice.

They left for Spain via London and Paris and crossed the Franco/Spanish border on December 14th. While in London, Ryan had togged himself out in military attire, leather jacket, army boots and leggings. As the late Frank Edwards jokingly remarked — 'Having told the boys to keep a low profile, he looked the real guerilla leader.'

On his return to London in September, Charlie began planning his departure to Spain. Ewart Milne remembers him coming into the offices of the Spanish Medical Aid Committee in New Oxford Street which were on the upper floor of the then Trade Union Club. He was waiting to go to Spain. He asked if he could help with the work and was referred to Milne by one of the typists. Milne was in charge of the operation of sending supplies of all kinds, including ambulances, to Spain. He was delighted to find that Charlie was from Dublin and that they both knew Leslie 'Yod' Daiken. Milne had nothing in the way of a job for Charlie although he suggested he could help out on a voluntary basis from time to time, but he succeeded in getting Charlie a job as a clerical assistant in the Boxers Union which had an office on the floor below. He took the job on the understanding that he might just suddenly 'disappear' at any time within the next few weeks or months.

His boss, who sympathised with the Republican cause, understood. In the weeks that followed Charlie and Milne became close friends. Charlie helped out with the work of Medical Aid and in their spare time they would wander around London and have cups of tea or coffee. Milne recalls —

> ... We had much in common and much to interest us, especially as we were both writing poetry. I don't remember, though, that during our night prowling and wanderings Charlie and myself ever disagreed on political matters. He was far more interested in military strategy than I was, he would talk for hours on the military strategy of the Peninsular Wars and give very critical assessments on Irish revoluntionary military tactics and strategy. I remember only once did he get annoyed with me, and that was when after reading a poem he had shown me, I said at least it was better than much of the romantic guff about 'Workers Arise' that was being written about the Spanish War. Charlie's blue eyes blazed and he shook his fine large head at me, saying, "For God's sake, you don't think I'm going out to Spain like a lot of those romantic fools, do you, Milne? You ought to know I'm going to study the military position and what has happened to military strategy in Spain since the Peninsular Wars, I've told you often enough."

His remark to Milne must be understood in the light of a natural irritation at being identified with the popular propaganda of the Third International and, secondly, he *was* seriously studying military strategy. Niall Sheridan says:

> ... He begun to study the theory of modern warfare. With uncompromising logic, he desired practical knowledge and felt that the Spanish Civil War afforded him an opportunity not to be missed.

And again, Montagu Slater says:

> Perhaps it was the study of Connolly's work on the technique of insurrection that revived Donnelly's interest in military science. I suspect it had always been there, though not always so lively. He was very much the Irishman in his awareness that behind all your laws and political theories, the final sanction is in arms. Once he had started seriously on military science, there was no stopping him. Everything led back to it. When Civil War broke out in Spain, he immediately began a military analysis.

The knowledge that he might suddenly be called to go to Spain did, as Slater said 'speed up the living process to some purpose'. As the threat to Madrid grew, he became increasingly restless. In the last few weeks in London, he wrote home to his friends in Dublin and sent several poems and short stores to Donagh MacDonagh for publication, most of which have been lost.

In December he made a flying visit home to say farewell to the family. Apart from my parents, my younger brother Anthony, who was then ten years old, was the only member of the family at home as we were all away at boarding school. However, he was able to visit my sister, Christine (Teenie) in Glasnevin and Anthony remembers going for a walk with Charlie to Drumcondra where he bought him a present of some toy soldiers and a book of childrens' poetry. Later that evening, he played 'soldiers' with Anthony.

In saying good-bye to my father, he mentioned that his work might take him abroad but that he shouldn't worry about him. He also said he was sorry for any trouble he had caused and my father let him know that all of that was in the past and forgotten and that he should tell Tom that he would be back in London in the New Year as promised.

In London, Tom, who was the only member of the family who knew that Charlie was going to Spain, told Charlie that he wanted to go with him. Charlie became angry saying that Tom knew that he was going for a specific purpose. It was bad enough to contemplate the effects on the family if anything were to happen to him but if both of them were to perish, it would be unthinkable.

Perhaps the most interesting surviving letters which he wrote home to friends during this time are his last two to Cecil ffrench Salkeld. In both he writes about poetry and its relation to politics. His letter dated 26th November 1936 reads:

> I'd very much like to hear what you think of the section of a poem I enclose. I'm very pleased with it because for the first time I've been able consciously to follow a technique and choose between ways of saying a thing. I like the alexandrine which seems to me about the best form of sustained work and one which leaves way for a good deal of subtlety. The trouble is that it's little suited to satire, that readiness to see limitations which I feel should be the stuffing of passion and emotion in poetry.
> The attitude of mind which goes for partisanship is surely the antithesis of that liable to produce poetry, whose richness of associations and highly specialised use of language is possible only to a completely detached mind, which doesn't mean a neutral or purblind one. Indeed, I can't imagine

really good poetry being produced in this year and age by anyone who is not intelligent enough to have worked out a very personally-felt and comprehensive philosophy. "Passionate pure and simple" is to-day more than ever liable to be taken for the opposite to what was (surely) meant by it . . .

In his last letter to Salkeld dated 21st December 1936, he makes the point more hurriedly but simply:

> I send you with this some work I've done lately. It looks as though I was developing a habit of sending my verse out, but it may be the last chance I'll have.
> There must be something in the instinct for perpetuation story. It's two years since I've written verse, and here I am now writing almost every day. If the fit doesn't leave me before I'm sent to Madrid I'll be meat for a bayonet shortly. I only wish I hadn't wasted the past two years. I wouldn't care if I'd written enough for one volume but I hate the idea of the world never hearing of so important a person! Never mind. You can't be a good poet if you're only interested in verse, at least, that's my view . . .

Charlie spent the last morning in London with Tom. In the afternoon he visited some friends and that night, the 23rd December, he left Victoria Station.

Montagu Slater recalled:

> I went to see him off on the last night. It was just before Christmas. At Victoria Station we found a young Irishman, another of his friends whose name I forget. We talked awkwardly as people do on railway stations. A youngster in a once-white sweater that washing had stretched down towards his knees, came up to say he was in charge of to-night's party. Would we please say good-bye here without going any nearer the platform barrier. Donnelly, like the others, was travelling with a week-end ticket to Paris to avoid using a passport. We said good-bye. Donnelly went off to his platform. The Irishman and I went for a drink. There didn't seem anything else to do.

CHAPTER FIVE

"Even the olives are bleeding."

When news of Charlie's departure for Spain became known to his friends, they were all saddened. Cora Hughes and George Gilmore had misgivings as had MacDonagh and Sheridan. In London Leslie Daiken was depressed while Ewart Milne was so affected that he quickly arranged to take the next lorry load of medical supplies to Madrid himself 'in order to see if I could meet up with him again.'

Volunteers for Spain were obliged to leave discreetly as their involvement in the Spanish Civil War was considered illegal as a result of the non-intervention pact. But Ed. Flaherty of the Abraham Lincoln Battalion which Charlie was to join later in Spain, considered that any government, U.S.A., British or French that didn't know what was going on would have had to be 'pretty dumb'. He recalls —

> I remember when we embarked for France from New York that cold day in January 1937, our little group from Boston, five in all, had been admonished the day before by those brilliant masters in the art of deception and guile, those so-called clever agents of the Communist International, that we would have to exercise the utmost caution as to our destination. So we stole down to the pier in a taxi and assembled on the dock prepared to sneak aboard only to find half a hundred other men gathered there waiting to help us sneak.

From Paris, Charlie and his group made their way south by train to the coastal town of Perpignan and from there to the Spanish border which they would have crossed on Christmas Day. They arrived at Albacete, headquarters of the International Brigades on the 27th December and moved on shortly afterwards to Madrigueras where the British Battalion were in training.

In January 1937, the formal organization of the International Brigades was begun by the third Communist International. Hitherto, volunteers from all over the world had been fighting on various fronts with various units, mainly French and German. Battalions were formed on the basis of language and there were five Brigades in all. The Eleventh Brigade was German, the Twelfth Italian anti-fascists, the Thirteenth was made up of Slavic speaking volunteers which included Poles and Czechs, the Fourteenth was French and Belgian and the Fifteenth Brigade was English speaking. Hence Irish volunteers together with English speaking survivors of the earlier fighting went into training with the British Battalion.

However, the situation into which Charlie arrived was far from satisfactory for the Irish Volunteers.

Frank Ryan, the acknowledged and popular leader of the Irish, had arrived at Albacete on the 16th December to find a total of 350 Irishmen, fifty being from Belfast, sixty Liverpool-Irish together with representatives from New York, Boston and Philadelphia. In addition, Irish volunteers who had enlisted at the beginning of hostilities were joining up with Ryan's men in the hope of forming an Irish Battalion. However, it would appear that an independent Irish Battalion was not acceptable to those who were organising the Battalions.

Shortly after his arrival, Ryan had sent an Irish Section of 43 men to the Cordoba Front with the British Company known as the Saklatvalas. 144 strong. They were so named after Saklatvala who was an Indian, born in Bombay, who became the first Communist M.P. to serve in the House of Commons. This Company was sent to augment the Marseillaise Battalion, the Franco-Belge, and was under the command of Capt George Nathan, an Englishman, with whom Ryan got on very well. He had served under the Crown forces in Ireland in 1920/21 but afterwards he became a Socialist. By all accounts, he was a very professional officer and was popular with the men. Before leaving, Nathan gave a short speech in which he thanked Frank Ryan for his assistance in organising the Company and Ryan praised Nathan for agreeing to the formation of an Irish section.

Joe Monks, who was a member of that section, wrote in his memoir — "With the Reds in Andalusia", of the amazement of the Irish at the appointment of Kit Conway as Section Commander instead of Frank Ryan, although Conway was himself popular. They were also surprised that Frank Ryan was not going with them to the front. He explained that there were matters to be taken care of in respect of the position of the Irish.

Meanwhile, back at Albacete, a conference was called by the Commander of the International Brigades, André Marty, a Frenchman, for the purpose of discussing the policy of the International Brigades' first military action. Marty was an enthusiastic disciple of Stalin and in addition to his position as Commander, was also a member of the Comintern Executive. According to Hugh Thomas's "Spanish Civil War": "By 1936 he had become obsessed with fear of Fascist or Trotskyist spies," and "he was arrogant, incompetent and cruel."

The conference delegates were from almost every country in the world and represented the best in the progressive movements,

Socialists, Republicans, Liberals, Communists, intellectuals and trade unionists.

During the conference, Frank Ryan complained of the political treatment of the Irish volunteers. Marty called him to order but, being hard of hearing, Ryan went on with his objections. Marty lost his temper but Ryan still went on, encouraged by some of the delegates from Ireland, America, Britain and Canada. Whereupon four guards proceeded to arrest Ryan, causing an uproar. That night, armed deputations sought Ryan's release unaware that he had been set free two hours after the conference ended.

Subsequently Ryan was sent to the Twelfth Italian and German Brigades in Madrid, supposedly for a week, which became a month. While he was away, some of the Irish had trouble with the British. The cause of the tension is not quite clear but when Ryan returned, he found that changes had occurred and, as he mentions in a letter to his friend, Gerald O'Reilly, 'I was told a pack of lies'. He also says in this letter, 'The representatives of the British CP wrecked the Irish Unit,' which he had hoped to keep intact. He goes on, 'I had a Dubliner named Terry Flanagan (fresh from Dublin Brigade, I.R.A.) in charge of that Section. Flanagan was framed as a 'suspect' and 'was being deported as an undesirable'. He had reached Barcelona on his way out. I stopped the deportation and got Flanagan back.' (Flanagan was later killed at the Front).

Peter O'Connor, who became a loyal friend of Charlie's and who, throughout the war, held the record for being the Irishman who came unhurt through the most engagements, remembers that a number of the Irish group were not at home with the British, and wanted to join the American Abraham Lincoln Battalion. A meeting was held to discuss the problem on January 12th. Peter O'Connor's diary records:

> At that meeting Charlie Donnelly, Johnny Power and myself fought very hard to be sent to the British Battalion. The main reason given by those who were for going to the Americans was because of the wrongs done to the Irish by the English in the past. They claimed that, though they were anti-fascist, they still looked on the English as the enemy. We, and here I mention Charlie Donnelly in particular, pleaded passionately for a distinction to be made between anti-fascist working class comrades from England and British Imperialism. It was an understandable, historical but political mistake that the vote went against us by such a small majority —five votes.

So some forty-five Irish volunteers joined the American Abraham Lincoln Battalion, and with some Irish-Americans and Irish-Canadians formed the James Connolly Centuria. They moved to Villanueva de la Jara where the Americans were training. The Irish-Americans welcomed them with open arms. Peter O'Connor, the Power brothers, all from Waterford, Mick Kelly and Charlie were among the Irish while Paul Burns, the Flaherty brothers, Ed., Charlie and Frank of Boston were among the Irish-Americans. In the words of Charlie Flaherty —"it was a day of strength".

Captain Mick Kelly, from Ballinasloe, who had worked with Charlie in London, was in charge of training the Irish Section and took it at a strenuous pace so that, at the end of a day's churning through the red soil in the fields and olive groves, the men welcomed an opportunity to relax and talk. Paul Burns recalls:

> The number one man was Charles Donnelly who joined us sometimes when we would skip the evening meal at the battalion Mess Hall to eat a more flavourful supper in one of the homes in the village. Conversation covered all aspects of the war in Spain and the various versions of the war as served up in the press of Ireland, England and the United States. We were all interested in the Irish Republican Congress which 'Charlie D' (D for Donnelly) to differentiate from 'Charlie O' (O'Flaherty) was able to elaborate. We talked about writers but at the time none of us knew that the blond young Irishman with the smiling blue eyes, who spoke so engagingly, had published poetry of rare merit.
>
> There were times when Charlie D could not join our evening gatherings because he had some things to do, some letters to write —. It was only later that we learned that his writing was not confined to correspondence, and that after slogging through the red mud all day, he was making the most of the time that remained before "lights out" to complete unfinished work in progress.

Paul Burns himself was a writer and columnist in America and a large proportion of the Lincolns were students.

Charlie, in his letters home to my brother Tom and to his friends, was cheerful. He was impressed with the Spanish people and in his last letter to Tom dated the 6th February he wrote:

> I've seen villages so small that there was no stationery shop and of indescribable poverty even now, when the whole fruit of the land is theirs, the kiddies without boots while we felt cold with good boots, the majority of the menfolk apparently earning a living as muleteers, and crowning the village in each case a church nearly as big as the Pro-Cathedral in Dublin. And what grand people — simple, kindly, and

intelligent. Like country people in Ireland. Only you feel that a great weight which they have borne for a long time has been thrown off and they feel the relief. You get a new impression that the entire community is involved in the business of organising public life, everybody interested and everybody enthusiastic. To go about among them gives you new courage — one day the Irish will be like this! . . . If they (the Irish people) knew the truth now they'd be with us and Dublin wouldn't be big enough to hold the complacent and well fed clergymen who libel the magnificent poor of Spain.

He goes on in this letter to pay a tribute to his comrades —

I see that the conservatives in England have been, as one would expect, misrepresenting the English volunteers and I daresay the same thing has been happening in Ireland. I would be glad if you could make this known. I have seen nearly all our lads out here. There's not been a dud amongst them. All have turned out good, and no-one regrets coming here. We are prouder to fight for the Spanish workers even more than when we were coming out, not only because we have seen with our own eyes, but because most of us have established personal relations here and number Spanish anti-fascists, men and women, among our dearest friends.

In particular, he paid tribute to Tommy Patton from Achill Island, whom he had known and who had been killed while defending Madrid in December, 1936. He was one of the first Irishmen to be killed.

Only lately I heard the details about Tommy Patton's death. He died covering the retiral of his group, with his head blown in and the rifle burst in his hands. Well, a man who has shown the courage of his Socialist convictions in Achill Island might be expected, when the necessity came, to put up so good a fight to the finish. If we all prove as good men as Tommy, we will have done our bit for the freedom of our own people, even though some of them repudiate us to-day.

He wrote about the pro-Franco propaganda in the Irish media and was scathing in his remarks:

I know how you feel, Tom, about the pro-Franco propaganda — out here I have at least the consolation of being able to promise myself that I'll bring a fascist down for every one of their dirty lies at which I used to be so annoyed. When you see the reality, the hectic propaganda of the Independent becomes as ludricous as annoying. Didn't that section of the press ever remind you of the swarms of beetles which scurry around when you lift a mossy stone and let in the light, fat, well-fed, and for all their middle-agedness, without the slightest knowledge of real life — except how to get the better of the next man.

He goes on to say that he is in good health, having escaped all the normal complaints. He then asks Tom to give Cora his address and sends her a message that if anything should happen 'I have always felt towards her as a very good friend', thus indicating that their relationship was not, then, what it had been, before he left Dublin for London. However, George Gilmore was to say that Cora's last thoughts before she died of tuberculosis three years later, were of Charlie. In the final paragraph of his long letter, he spoke of the family:

All that worries me is how you and my father and mother feel about me. Don't worry, old boy, we'll be talking about all this together one day. Please tell me when you write what is the position at home, and what I should do, and meanwhile do whatever you think right to prevent their having any cause for worry. I know how they feel about my politics, but I hope that one day we will all be happy together.

Training continued amid speculation as to when rifles would be issued which was thought to be during the second and final phase. Little they knew that phase two of their training would be eliminated out of necessity and that their baptism of fire was imminent.

On February 6th (when Charlie had written his last letter home), Franco's forces launched an offensive in the Jarama Valley, backed up fully by Italian and German troops, units of the Spanish Foreign Legion and Moorish troops plus air cover.

The Fascist objective was to cut the Madrid to Valencia road, so to encircle and capture Madrid.

When the Lincolns received orders to go to the Front on February 15th, they had achieved a strength of approx. 450 men, divided into two infantry companies, a machine-gun company, a medical unit together with service units. Their uniform consisted of heavy shoes with woolen khaki-coloured outfits, woolen khaki beret which could be worn beneath a helmet. A black rubberised raincoat completed the outfit.

They were moved by trucks to Madrigueras where rifles, bayonets, helmets, ammunition belts and ammunition (150 rounds to a man) were issued. They moved on slowly and as much as possible under darkness, stopping on the 16th February at Chinchon, where their Commander, Capt. Robert Merriman reported to General Gal,

Commander of the Thirty-fifth Division, that the battalion was ready for action. Captain Robert Hale Merriman was the first commander of the Lincoln Battalion. Born of Scottish-American parents, he was twenty-eight years old when he arrived in Spain. A graduate of Nevada University, he had held the post of head teaching assistant at the University of California. He was later promoted to the rank of Major. The character portrayed by Gary Cooper in the screen version of Hemingway's "For Whom the Bell Tolls" was based on Merriman. Before they moved on to Morata de Tajuna, Capt. Merriman obtained permission for the battalion to stop on the way to enable each man to shoot five rounds into the surrounding hills, as the rifles were still packed with grease and had not been used. Along the way, the men dismounted from the trucks and cleaned the newly issued rifles with whatever came to hand, in many cases the tails of their shirts were used. Then they lined up along the road and each man fired several shots into the hills on either side. This was to be the only practice the battalion would have before going into battle.

The British Battalion had gone into action on the 12th February by which time the fascists had broken through the lines and crossed the Jarama River at two points. In heavy fighting on the 12th, Franco's forces advanced somewhat but were repulsed by the Republicans with severe losses. Among those killed was Kit Conway. Frank Ryan was wounded. At this point four International Battalions were engaged in fighting — The British, The Dimitroff, The Thaelmann and the Franco-Belge.

When the Lincolns reached field headquarters, they moved across a railway track and up a hill which became known to them as Suicide Hill. Capt. John Scott, an Englishman whose real name was Inver Marlowe and who was the Commander of the 1st Infantry Company led the Irish Section of the Company to the west of the hill, where they were to remain until the 20th February. The Irish Section's Commander was Bill Henry of Dublin who had taken over from Capt. Michael Kelly, who had been left behind to bring up new units of volunteers.

On February 23rd, the Lincoln Battalion moved into the attack, spearheaded by the James Connolly Section. This attack was intended as a show of strength and was an attempt to stop the insurgent offensive. This was their first time over the top. Paul Burns described the scene:

> Our attack began late in the afternoon and the advance continued into the night over a field dotted by occasional olive trees and a stubble of ancient gnarled grape vines as thick as a man's arm. The men advanced by

crawling and, where the scant cover permitted, by short dashes.

In one of those interludes beneath an olive tree, I looked around. On my left was Charlie Donnelly . . . a few yards away, in a shallow scoop of earth was Capt. Scott with Frank Flaherty, his aide.

Charles Donnelly joined me under the olive tree. We fired until our rifles burned in our hands with scarcely a word between us, besides 'Hi, Charlie, how's it goin'? and the reply, 'Pretty good, how's the rest of the boys?' Later, in the darkness, we became separated and I never saw him again.

Paul Burns was wounded that night and was sent to hospital. He returned to the front on the 1st of March.

This attack was to fail because in a confused situation which developed, troops on the Americans' left flank held back. Capt. Merriman, realising the position, ordered the men to return to their original positions. Capt. John Scott was killed in this action, and Bill Henry succeeded him as Commander.

Ed. Flaherty later recalled the aftermath of the battle —

> You have heard the expression 'strong men wept and weak men did something or other', well, most of the men left, felt as I did, hopeless, helpless, hungry and cold. We had no idea where the enemy was, in front, bullets came from the sides, in back, who knew, not our leaders we were sure, for nobody came near us. Orders came down the trench from man to man. But Charlie D. grinned at me when I greeted him and we sat in our misery, joking about the mess our betters had got us into.

However, compared to the attack which was to follow on the 27th, this was only a light skirmish.

The following night, the Lincolns were moved to a new position from which, three days later, the attack of the 27th February was to be launched.

This attack's objective was to take the rebel trenches, move the enemy back in the direction of the Jarama River, three kilometers away, and, ultimately, to drive them back across the river itself. The men were told that they would be supported by Republican tanks and planes. However, when the planes did appear, they could not tell whether they were rebel or Republican. The Lincolns were to go over the top only when the Twenty-fourth Spanish Brigade, occupying adjacent positions, had come in line with them. The Americans began the attack and the rifles and machine guns of the Twenty-fourth Brigade were heard nearby. But they never advanced very far. Brigade HQ then ordered the Americans to go over alone. Capt. Merriman argued that the attack could not succeed but after some debate, he was overruled and the order to attack was given. Capt. Merriman himself was among the first casualties. Wave after wave went over charging the fascist lines which were only 150 metres away. They found themselves in a field dotted with fire-scarred olive trees. It was in this engagement that Charlie was to die. A member of the Canadian Mackenzie-Papineau which was part of the Abraham Lincoln Battalion, recalled the scene:

> The firing becomes heavier. Ahead of us you can see the ground completely covered with spurts of dust. They are concentrating their fire on the left and right flank and straight ahead. From all directions. We run for cover. Charles Donnelly, Commander of the Irish Company, is crouched behind an olive tree. He has picked a bunch of olives from the ground and is squeezing them. I hear him say quietly, during a lull of machine-gun fire "Even the olives are bleeding". A bullet got him square in the temple a few minutes later. He is buried there now underneath the olives.

(In this passage, Charlie is named as Commander of the Irish Company. In the absence of confirmation, it is a matter for speculation that Charlie may have assumed command following the death of Bill Henry, who was also killed that day.)

Of the 450 men who had gone to the front with the Lincolns, 127 were killed and 200 were wounded.

Ed. Flaherty, described the following morning:

> The morning of the 28th finally dawned after a hideous night of fear and helplessness. Groans and cries could be heard from the battlefield. Were they fascist? Were they our men? Would the enemy attack, now that we were leaderless and broken? All that night we peered into the darkness waiting for the counter-attack that didn't come.

Although the survivors were sure that the attack had failed, it had not. This attack of 27th February had apparently shown the fascists that the Jarama front was too heavily defended. The Republican forces held the position until the end of the war.

Charlie died at the age of 22, ten years to the day after the death of his mother. His comrades thought he was 26 but he had falsified his age on enlistment. Even in death, he went too far . . . his body was found 10 days later, he had almost penetrated enemy lines. He was carried down the mountainside by three members of the Republican Congress, the Power brothers, Peter and Johnny, and Peter O'Connor. He was buried beneath an olive tree in the Jarama Valley. Edwin Rolfe, in "The Lincoln Battalion" described Charlie as "the most original talent in the entire battalion", following the discovery of two of his poems among his papers. The two poems, The Tolerance of Crows and Poem were pasted up on the Battalion notice board, outlined in black.

Josephine Herbst, the American jounalist and writer, and one of the few women Correspondents allowed at the front during the Spanish Civil War, wrote in her journal:

> Charles Donnelly (poet) 26 years univ. grad. killed Feb. 27. Body found very close to fascist lines. Body stinking after 10 days. Brought in. Face fresh and naive looking.

Alan McLarnon, formerly doubting the physical courage of intellectuals, who fought beside Charlie in the line and got back wounded, told Leslie Daiken afterwards:

> Charlie was the surprise of the whole action to us. Listen, his pluck was terrific. And very real. He couldn't have felt anything, it came so fast. I tell you, he just didn't know what hit him.

Ewart Milne went to Madrid with the next consignment of Medical supplies and went straight to the Headquarters of the XV Brigade to enquire about Charlie. There he found Frank Ryan who informed him of Charlie's death. He writes:

> You can imagine my sense of shock and distress. After all I had followed Charlie out as quickly as I could, without actually joining the Brigade, and already, he was dead.

Cora Hughes and George Gilmore were grief stricken. George Gilmore was to relate a strange incident which happened to him after Charlie's death. Apparently, while he was going upstairs to Cora Hughes's flat in Wicklow Street, he suddenly felt what he thought was someone's hand on his shoulder. Looking round, there was nobody there but he sensed Charlie's presence. Within a few days, he was to hear of Charlie's death.

Deeply affected, Charlie's friends in Dublin, Donagh MacDonagh, Blanaid Salkeld, Cecil Salkeld, David Clarke all wrote poems in tribute to him, as did Ewart Milne.

However, the one most affected was my father. Unaware that Charlie was fighting in Spain, he had, as promised, gone back to London in early February 1937 to help Tom set up a business. He bought the interest in the lease of a shop in Isleworth and Tom commenced business. He was very optimistic about the venture and remained in London for several weeks. Just as everything seemed to be going right, Tom had a letter from Johnny Power telling him of Charlie's death. Tom had the difficult task of breaking the news to my father.

At first, my father cried like a baby but soon became angry. He was so distressed that Tom rushed out and brought a priest home to talk to him and console him. My father was comforted but in the light of the harsh preaching of the day, he was haunted by the thought that Charlie was damned, soul and body. He used to visit the local church in Isleworth each day and just sit there, unable even to pray. He told me later as he sat in the Church one day, he had a wonderful experience... He had a vision of my mother coming from the right hand side of the altar, while Charlie came from the left. They joined hands in the centre and both smiled at him. He was amazed and at that moment, he recalled, the heavy weight that had descended upon him when he had first heard the news of Charlie's death, suddenly lifted and he felt free. He was convinced that Charlie was with my mother and had found the ultimate Truth.

L. to r., Joseph Donnelly and father, after Charlie's death 1937.

ON FIRST HEARING JOHN COUNT McCORMACK

From out the stillness, accents sweet arise,
Sweet accents, accents tender so!
Sweet accents fill my ears, my senses o'erpower,
Sweet accents fill my heart and overflow!
Sweet accents, sweeter than e'en Orpheus raised I wist
For man-made lute could never equal this —
                                      God's own creation!

Each moment, more divinely sweeter growing,
Those thrilling tender tones ascend
Until in climax of rare heavenly harmony
With kindred seraph notes they blend
What sickly soul does not that glorious voice inspire!
My breast, my heart, my soul, my very being takes fire!
                                      Trembling elation!

To me it seems the world is far behind,
The cruel world, so cruelly drear!
Now in a heaven of song divine I dwell
And now an Angel's voice I hear —
Such voice as surely Shepherds heard in Bethlehem,
When Christ came down on earth to die for men!
                                      Sweet Reparation!

Or has from Heaven an Angel voice come down
To compensate with brief, too beauteous song
The misery of long dreary toilsome days!
— Soon will I waking, find the Angel gone
His sweet song ended, and his sweet voice still!
My earthly heaven shattered; the harsh world once more chill.
                                      O Lamentation!

The song has ceased, and from the vaulting dome
The stilled voice, the echoes doth recall!
The song has ceased; its rapture still remains.
Though all is silent in the lofty hall.

DA MIHI

1
Give me thy speed, wild wailing Wind,
Thy never-ending speed be me!
That I may fly
Into the embrace of the sky,
Into the bosom of wild eyed eternity,
Eternity, whose darkness is an eye!
That I may cleave,
May, wild-souled, cleave
The shoreless waters of unending night,
That I may be
What human ne'er has been,
Wild spirit, bodiless and free,
Wild singing spirit of breast-bursting might!

2
Give me thy hotness, molten Sun,
Thy melting hotness be my soul!
That I may burn
An unquenched light;
That I may conquer
Deep-shouldered night;
That a star, shining bright,
I may be
Above the tumbling mountains of a night-cloaked sea,
Above the soul-strewn waters of eternity!
That my song-laden bark
May conquer the Dark,
That, girded in splendour, I may reach the goal!

3
Give me thy redness, love-sighing Rose,
Thy blushing tenderness be my heart!
That I may feel,
May, love-taught, feel
My fellow-creatures' woe;
That my song may be kind,
My verse warm, lined
With truth such as angels know;
That my youth-written book
Be a crystal brook
For the parched soul to drink deep!
As sweet as soft-shouldered nymphs' backward look,
From the fading island of rose-embowered sleep!

THE DEATH SONG

Burst from my breast, O my song, sweet song,
Like a gold tongued blast, O my song, sweet song,
Like a gold tongued blast, O my song, sweet song,
Burst from me, and let me die!
For hate must die, and fear must die
And sorrow is not in the sky,
But tho' God crack Eternity
        Love lives on!
This life is but a walking sleep
Above a dark unwanted Deep,
Then waken soul, and wildly leap,
        And Life is won!
Burst forth my song to Eternity,
And thunder like the cave lunged sea,
And I, my song, will follow thee,
        Will follow thee!
Will follow thee, will follow thee!
My song, thro' all Eternity,
My love-made soul will pale Death flee,
        And follow thee!
And if love cannot live in life,
Then Death embrace, and leave the strife,
And take Eternity to wife,
        And live in Death!
All live in Death, whose life was Love,
Whose Love was pure as the Vast Above,
Whose heart was eagle, whose heart was dove,
        I'll live in Death!
I'll live in Death, a spirit free,
A cool voiced mountain wind I'll be,
And thou, my love, will come to me,
        To love in Death!
To love in Death, to love for ever,
In Death, warm love grows cooler never,
And Death's pale eyes can never sever
        Who love in Death!
        Who love in Death!

TO YOU

In the old days of bitter faces
And cold eyes,
I would go to the lone, large places, the hills
And the skies,
To the twilight of grey, great shadows
And bird cries . . .
And shadows would hide me, and the wind sighed
With my sighs . . .
But you, my Jewess, having come, and gone,
Whence can I bring my soul,
When the winds but mock, and the shadows
Bring mirrors of thy soul?

AT THE DREAMING OF THE DREAMS

My dreams are dreaming, and the sacred books
Have closed their lips, and smothered up their lies,
And all the worlds are whirling in the skies,
And all the skies are like a woman's looks.

I live, I live, and yet I reck it not
I am one with the depths and with the heights,
I am beyond the fadings of the lights
Of all the suns. I live, and yet live not.

The murmur of the waters of all Being
Is me; the silence of undying Death.
Eternity breathes in me, and its breath
Is Death in hand with Life, Unbeing with Being.

The bosom of God's parent, boundless Sleep,
Enfolds me, and I drown within the eyes,
The smiling eyes that are a woman's eyes,
The eyes of all the soul of all the Deep.

And all the dreamings of the dreams of God
Are burning from me, like a woman's love,
I fade and melt in Space, below, above,
And God is in my being, I in God.

Oh, all men's toil to prove true the great lie
Of the world, like staring in a sea
To find the secret of its blue, while He
Above, reflects it from the waters of His eye.

Oh, all the world is but an endless lie,
Eternity and Space a swirling dream.
My soul is like the murmur of a stream.
I dream within a dream. To live, to die,
To be, or not to be, matters not, dream I.

THE PROFESSOR

His soul genteelly pants for heaven
Though not uncomfortable here;
And one by one he counts the sixty-seven
References to nature in King Lear.

His soul on which he lays much stress
Admires the Higher Things of Life,
Going to God he makes progress
Through lyric Cry and Wedded Wife.

He has ideals, such as Democracy,
His epithets have good authority,
Sparing of body and of soul —
An argument for Birth Control.

TO A BAD CRITIC
*(Who reproached a friend of mine, a good
poet, with obscurity).*

"Words strung in grotesque patterns,
Meaningless and passionless," you say,
"True passion is spontaneous as the day."
"This is but poetry and passion faked."
Some day you will get sense — Till then,
That if a beautiful goddess walked 'mong men,
'Twere unwise that she go naked.
Consider that,
Impertinent brat,
In the hope that 'twill add
To the small stock that is under your hat.

THE DEAD
With apologies to – Myself

What ghastly sight is this, within the Hall
A row of tombstones lined along the wall.
Ah, here they lie, the Muse's valiant slain,
Of that brave band, does not one soul remain?
There does. See lone O'Phelan, mourning in the Main.
E'en as I look, he raises his lorn head,
And thus makes sad lament above the Dead:
'Of late a faction rose with much uproar,
Turning their heads — which had been turned before —
But, ah, their little day was quickly o'er . . .' —
(Praised be the Lord! say I, between my sighs).
But deaf in grief, O'Phelan said: 'Here lies
Caomhighin, who held, the dignity of our sex
In stride abides not, but in hornrimmed specs,
For with their aid — I libel the anoint —
He could see everything (except the point)!
Cox, who lies here, at rhetoric adept,
Raged at his audience, while his audience slept;
While he waxéd wroth about Freemasonry
The ladies amorous waxed ('bout buns and tea).
Here Barnabas was thrown, whose Muse being lame,
He mistook notoriety for fame;
Loved of the ladies, as orator had he
Every gift — save that of orat'ry;
But, ah, although we smiled whene'er he 'spoke'
We smiled not when he joked — that was no joke!
Our J.F.K. lies here, whose pen, my lad,
Had tons of dignity ('twas all it had);
Champion he was, and champion resplendent,
Of faith, and morals, and the 'Independent'.
Now he lies here, along with many more,
Who were a merry company of yore
And raised dust and the devil in Sixth-Four.
. . . ."
I left him there, my eyes with tears being blind,
To write about it to the "Catholic Mind."

IN A LIBRARY

Are the moods voiceless? For I have no words.
Blood cannot talk, although it crack the skin.
Red hots and colds are pumped up from the pit
Like hungering men; and no word-woman being near, sink again
    howling in.
And I fume, and look outside on the grey
Wind hammered to fantasy day.

STASIS

1
The silent light descends
Like a cloth over me
Here under the trees
Whose presence has infolded on itself
And the monotone
Of the afar-falling waters pours over my mind.
The rising thoughts level before it
And as seeds borne by the wind
Are borne away from me.
Thoughts go. Thoughts bend, break, float away.

2
This is a sleeping place,
A cast shell
Of the snail of the world,
A thing left in a crevice.

SMALL BIRDS SEEN THROUGH TENUOUS TREES

Small birds seen through tenuous trees
spin out in flickering Time a
past scent of hay, dew on the cold gate-lock.
On the reach of a tactile prong
is superimposed a line of Keats.
The soul of Mr. Powell purrs
among the kerbstones' interstices
which raise it toward an image-synthesis.
Between the quality of female fingers
and its ramifications
his soul appraises its delicate oscillations.

O in the globed air of a thought-fusion
how satisfying
a sun-spurted series of ledges
a match box,
a foot
springing.
Through streets and the well-considered trees
("No too elaborate tapestries
let just the gesture, the emphasis"),
Mr. Powell's subtle soul
propels finely.
"The thin fine thread of my desire"
vaguely consummated on a garden wall
(Three blades of grass and red dust).
"How thrilling, and, indeed, a quite valid emotion".

APPROACH

The tightening eyes, tendrilled of sympathy,
The accepted secret before a third;
The unrequired gesture, imperfect denial of contact.

The flaunt, the posture, display of the self,
Under appraisal relenting to seriousness,
And sudden tenderness lightening in simple actions;

The gaze, responded to, steadying in brave request;
Prolonged at acceptance; the attitude
Breaking in mutual and offered laughter.

MR. SHERIDAN'S MORNING PRAYER

At my rising up I pray
For a middling fine day,
For an adequate reply
From the manna-dropping sky,
For a fire to warm my shins
When the evening light begins,
For a pint or two to quaff,
For a robustious belly laugh,
For a walk with other bards,
Of upwards of a hundred yards;
Send these blessing, pure and small,
On myself, and on us all.

STORY: WRITTEN IN DEPRESSION AT A DEBATE ON THE ESSENCE OF POETRY

Bang
down the riverside
extenuating circumstances while temporarily insane
why did his wife?

Angry words to false emotions often lead astray
I have been lead away.
Requiescat.

MUSIC, NICE TURNS OF THOUGHT

Music, nice turns of thought, insert
(But cannot send it out in flower)
Among distended meshes of desire.
Salt beauty spilled from you inlays the world;
But no bright, humming image can absorb
The acid, burning, burning your image for me.

Ah, your soft qualities prick hard, my love,
The body breaks in crystals of desire.

Why is there so much urgency
In bodily grace?
Why is the daring posture, winning movement of dance
Uncancellable by ignorance?
We all know the man
To music deaf, he says:
But can he, or she, or we resist
The animal compelling embrace
Of ardent Dance
Sunny as Summer's hazy, golden gaze.
The clinging tread
Foot kissing earth as loth to leave
Sucks honey from the ground,
Bereaves earth in a bound
Or, whishing, a futile leaf
Autumn-hooted is jibed
By every stringy gust of orchestra . . .

WAGES OF DEVIATION

Diffident labour of poetry,
perilous pleasure of the tightened mind,
youth's lonely, austere joy
were broken by your hands
bringing elation, opening
through the white summer roads, the world.

Through love's complications we,
intricacy of touch and speech —
when touch acquired the delicacy of speech
and speech invaded apprehending flesh —
wove, wove together.

Life and a game between us,
through uninterrupted years,
we dreamed
under the twilit trees, when broke
the questing labour of desire,
in intimacy on the blood.

Now there's resentment, purpose crossed,
heart's outcry of tears in the street,
contracted heart distorts the world.
Or, truce declared, your memory,
hair blown fine against lamplight, makes
my heart and hands go wild.

UNNOTICED IN HURRY OF CALLOUS GOOD-BYE

Unnoticed in hurry of callous good-bye,
Kindness of one with own troubles is squandered
On smile disrespectful lingering on kerb
And strained nose-bridge of preoccupations.

Who welcomes the plan-filled arrival at stations,
For no ulterior reason is busied,
And through a year suffers, unarmed for aloofness,
A steady deterioration of response.

Eyes lose aliveness for his implications,
Assenting motions, daily dull their
Quality, interest moving to a third
Leaving him for private thoughts' invasion.

THE FLOWERING BARS

After sharp words from the fine mind,
protest in court,
the intimate high head constrained,
strait lines of prison, empty walls,
a subtle beauty in a simple place.

There to strain thought through the tightened brain,
there weave
the slender cords of thought, in calm,
until routine in prospect bound
joy into security,
and among strictness sweetness grew,
mystery of flowering bars.

THE TOLERANCE OF CROWS

Death comes in quantity from solved
Problems on maps, well-ordered dispositions,
Angles of elevation and direction;

Comes innocent from tools children might
Love, retaining under pillows,
Innocently impales on any flesh.

And with flesh falls apart the mind
That trails thought from the mind that cuts
Thought clearly for a waiting purpose.

Progress of poison in the nerves and
Discipline's collapse is halted.
Body awaits the tolerance of crows.

POEM

Between rebellion as a private study and the public
Defiance, is simple action only on which will flickers
Catlike, for spring. Whether at nerve-roots is secret
Iron, there's no diviner can tell, only the moment can show.
Simple and unclear moment, on a morning utterly different
And under circumstances different from what you'd expected.

Your flag is public over granite. Gulls fly above it.
Whatever the issue of the battle is, your memory
Is public, for them to pull awry with crooked hands,
Moist eyes. And village reputations will be built on
Inaccurate accounts of your campaign. You're name for orators,
Figure stone-struck beneath damp Dublin sky.

In a delaying action, perhaps, on hillside in remote parish,
Outposts correctly placed, retreat secured to wood, bridge mined
Against pursuit, sniper may sight you carelessly contoured.
Or death may follow years in strait confinement, where diet
Is uniform as ceremony, lacking only fruit.
Or on the barrack square before the sun casts shadow.

Name, subject of all-considered words, praise and blame
Irrelevant, the public talk which sounds the same on hollow
Tongue as true, you'll be with Parnell and with Pearse.
Name aldermen will raise a cheer with, teachers make reference
Oblique in class, and boys and women spin gum of sentiment
On qualities attributed in error.

Man, dweller in mountain huts, possessor of coloured mice,
Skilful in minor manual turns, patron of obscure subjects, of
Gaelic swordsmanship and mediaeval armoury.
The technique of the public man, the masked servilities are
Not for you. Master of military trade, you give
Like Raleigh, Lawrence, Childers, your services but not yourself.

HEROIC HEART

Ice of heroic heart seals plasmic soil
Where things ludicrously take root
To show in leaf kindess time had buried
And cry music under a storm of 'planes,
Making thrust head to slacken, muscle waver
And intent mouth recall old tender tricks.
Ice of heroic heart seals steel-bound brain.

There newer organs built for friendship's grappling
Waste down like wax. There only leafless plants
And earth retain disinterestedness.
Thought, magnetised to lie of the land, moves
Heartily over the map wrapped in its iron
Storm. Battering the roads, armoured columns
Break walls of stone or bone without receipt.
Jawbones find new ways with meat, loins
Raking and blind, new ways with women

FRAGMENT 1

Fastbound to a million dreaming limbs,
The fabric of our culture swells.
It's securely founded on cancelling whims
Unshaken when one of its pillars turns
In rhythms, and unsure eyes
Memory soon returns.

Fastbound to a million insect limbs,
The fabric of our culture swells;
It's securely founded on cancelling whims

The surprise rush spiked out to relevance,
Twenty pictures per second make writing,
Twenty mens actions make sense.

FRAGMENT 2

Rum for cargo and civilisation for ballast
The ships of state cross the briny ocean
This man sees his own future or
Because he liked luxurious surroundings
Or grew excited to talk to a pen at the place,
Or mainly took pleasure in the tricks
Of the trade, put his weight to the communal
Wheel.

Over the ocean cross the ships of state,
Cargo rum and ballast civilisation.

FRAGMENT 3

If you must let the fabric decay
Of reason and discernment,
The threads of life fly loose.

With tired eyes, so sending
Adrift a cargo meant
For a different ending.

NOTES ON THE POEMS

"*On First Hearing John Count McCormack*": unpublished; written 1929 in Mountjoy Square; age, 15 years. Source: Sr Mary Carmel (Aunt), Holy Faith Convent.
"*Da Mihi*": his first published poem, published in Comhthrom Feine, November 1931.
"*The Death Song*": this poem is included in a prose piece of the same name in Comhthrom Feine, December 1931.
"*To You*": published in Comhthrom Feine, April 1932.
"*At the Dreaming of the Dreams*": published in The National Student, May 1932.
"*The Professor*": previously unpublished. Source Leslie Daiken, via Cecil ffrench Salkeld. Written sometime during 1932. Reference to King Lear forms part of an essay 'Literature in Ireland', published in Comhthrom Feine in May 1933: "The chief critical discoveries of the past year in University College (Dublin) are not difficult to number. There is, first of all, the momentous discovery that 'King Lear' contains sixty-seven referenes to nature, and the appropriate moral drawn from this and other facts in the play."
"*To a Bad Critic*": Published in Comhthrom Feine, May 1932.
"*The Dead*": Published in Comhthrom Feine, 1932.
"*In A Library*": published in Motley, January 1933.
"*Stasis*": published in Comhthrom Feine, November 1933.
"*Small Birds Seen Through Tenuous Trees*": published in Comhthrom Feine, March 1934.
"*Approach*": published in Comhthrom Feine, April 1934.
"*Mr. Sheridan's Morning Prayer*": published in Comhthrom Feine, May 1934. Refers to Niall Sheridan, fellow student and friend. Light-hearted in tone, it was written to fill in a gap in the magazine.
"*Story: Written in Depression at a Debate on the Essence of Poetry*": published Comhthrom Feine, May 1934.
"*Music, Nice Turns of Thought*": Written in 1934, previously unpublished. Source Leslie Daiken via Cecil ffrench Salkeld. Salkeld, in a letter to Daiken, claims the second verse had an input from himself as Charlie wrote the poem in Salkeld's studio one afternoon while Salkeld painted.
"*Wages of Deviation*": unpublished written 1935; there is a note by Montagu Slater on a copy of the original MS.: "This is the poem Charlie gave me to send to Eliot — F.M.S."
"*Unnoticed in Hurry of Callous Good-bye*": unpublished, written 1935. Source — Leslie Daiken.
The Flowering Bars": written while serving his last prison sentence, Jan. 1935; published in Goodbye Twilight, by Leslie Daiken, London 1936.
"*The Tolerance of Crows*": found among his papers at Jarama; a copy had been sent to Donagh MacDonagh for publication in Ireland To-Day; first published

there in February 1937; subsequently in The Lincoln Battalion by Edwin Rolfe; Poems for Spain, Spender & Lehman, pp 50/51. Written in London in 1936 prior to his departure for Spain.

"*Poem*": found among his papers at Jarama. Written in London in November 1936. A copy was sent to Donagh MacDonagh for publication in Ireland To-Day. First published there in January 1937. Subsequently published in The Lincoln Battalion by Edwin Rolfe, and in Romanceros de los Voluntarios de la Libertad 1937. Contains references to George Gilmore; the final 3 lines refer to Gilmore's refusal to join or support the new administration in 1932.

"*Heroic Heart*": written in Spain in February 1937. Original sent to Donagh MacDonagh for publication in Ireland To-Day. Published there in July 1937.

"*Fragment 1*": found among political notes; an incomplete and rough version of poem; written 1936 on reverse of manuscript of Charlie's book on Connolly.

"*Fragment 2*": written 1936, found on reverse of Ms of Charlie's book on Connolly.

"*Fragment 3*": written 1936; perhaps another part of Fragment 2; found on reverse of Ms on Connolly.

L. to r., Peter, Charlie, Joe; Summer 1931.

EWART MILNE

SONG OF THE NIGHT MARKET

Through the silent squares
The guitar tinkles loud.

> Do you remember Carlos, Maria?
> His kindly song
> To the balustrade rising,
> On the dubious calm
> Of the clear evening.
> Do you remember Carlos, Maria?
> Now the grandees are back in the castles.
>
> Dust is his death, Maria,
> His poet's blood rusts
> The spades of the labourers,
> Bending their backs
> In the fields of olive.
> Do you remember Carlos, Maria?
> Now that the grandees are back in the castles.

The guitar tinkles loud
Through the silent squares.

EWART MILNE

THINKING OF ARTOLAS

Sirs and Senoras, let me tell you a story,
A story neither of long ago nor faraway
But close enough now and to you unhappily.
We will call it Going-into-History
And you all know History is a cruel country
Where tiger terraces crouch drinking rivers waterless
And sheep immobilised by sombrero Shepherds' piping . . .
It could be set in Estremadura or Cordova,
Time crawling like inches and napoleonic wars
Dogeared in textbooks seeming the latest in strategy —
At least until recently. Or as Shaw might have said
The life force gets going but man has his lag . . .
True. And to gain on his lag must man lose his leg,
And truncate himself, as in Estremadura?

Well, at Casada's we ate ortolans elsewhere we drank coffee.
In the Gran Via in the Colon we went into conference.
All day the starlings on the Ramblas whispered,
All day the dead air pacified the street,
Fat pigeons swaggered on the Plaza Catalunya.
It was easy enough to analyse an ortolan,
Conjure pigeon into pie: translate con leche . . .

But the starlings worried me, and their whispering,
I could never understand their whispering.
It weaved breathlessly up and up like the Coulin —
Or like that dissonance outsoaring ecstacy, heard
Near any roadside or beside any bed, disrupting the
Lovers enlaced, singing with no sound and saying
'O the world is bright and empty.'

At Madrid we dined with the newspaper bunch.
So-and-So shouted they all called him a Fascist —
There *had* been whispers — but he didn't care
He shouted for Empire. That was alright
Empire shouted for him — one supposes, somewhere.
All day I was a method of analysis . . . Did my heart, Tomas,
Or your depthless eyes tell me analysis was cowardly
While los Madrilenos were barricading their old Madrid out?
. . . All day So-and-So the Fascist was blustering.
I analysed his quality as extreme
Scatology and efficiency walking backwards, with a shrug . . .
But sadly I knew the whispering starlings
Wintering would rise from the Plaza Catalunya
Before I returned.

With Jarama held they brought him in, the tankist.
From his Georgian hair the blood smiled through,
And smiled on the paving and from the verandah
Smiled as it dripped and adventured below . . .
In parks they dream of penny murder non-intervention —
He took the hammered blow and said Salud —
All day my heart with love was helpless, all day I knew
He had gone further than I towards finding a synthesis.
With Jarama held his wound wore on, the Georgian
Who held a dawnstar and not nettles as we do —
Whisper, starlings, whisper! Be incorruptible and saying
'O the world is bright and always living'.

Sirs and Senoras, let me end my story —
I show you earth, earth formally,
And Two on guard with the junipers.
Two, Gael and Jew side by side in a trench
Gripping antique guns to flick at the grasshoppers
That zoomed overhead and the moon was rocking.
Two who came from prisonment, Gael because of Tone,
Jew because of human love, the same for Jew as German —
Frail fragments both, chipped off and forgotten readily . . .

I set them together, Izzy Kupchik and Donnelly;
And of that date with death among the junipers
I say only, they kept it: and record the exploded
Spreadeagled mass when the moon was later
Watching the wine that baked earth was drinking.
Such my story, Sirs and Senoras. Whether you like it
Or pay a visit to your vomitorium, is all one . . .
Perhaps you'll like junipers and a moon steadied,
High baked earth and night's formalism,
Remembering that History is always a cruel country
And crueller man than April.

CECIL FFRENCH SALKELD

SOCCORO ROJO
for Charles Donnelly

So goodbye dreams
And silent midnight schemes
That wish world well:
A knell
Chilled steel with morning
Signals an early warning
Piercing each warm protesting cell
Jarring the skull
Rigid and dull
To rattle out bone's shattering farewell.

Cold obsession of thought:
Caught
Strung, hung, in barbed entanglements of hate,
Fate
Never cuts clean;
But shames and makes obscene
All that we loved:
Beauty that moved, allured,
Is not obscured,
But blurred and blotted on the slate.

I have seen brightness indeed
And headlong without heed
Paid all demands;
But now Death's ghost-bright tissue
Pursues and issues icy countermands;
Bans hazy seas and lands always sought:
I have been taught
To hazard night and day
This malleable, doom-eager clay
In alien but knowledgeable hands.

BLANAID SALKELD

CASUALTIES

Who would think the Spanish war
Flared like new tenure of a star,
The way our rhymes and writings are?
That Hilliard spilled his boxer's blood
Through Albacete's snow and mud,
And smiled to comrade death, Salud.
That Charlie Donnelly, small, frail,
And flushed with youth, was rendered pale —
But not with fear: in what queer squalor
Was smashed up his so ordered valour,
That rhythm, that steely earnestness,
That peace of poetry, to bless
Discordant thoughts of divers men —
Blue gaze that burned up lie and stain,
Put out by death.
I keep my breath:
So many grow upon my stem,
I cannot take their sap from them.
But to right charity, with spurs,
Through spite's asperity infernal —
My verity of verse
Is nothing else
But rattle of light shells
With no kernel,
Since Dublin boys have striven, and are
Knit to that alien soil, where war
Burns like the inception of a star.

DAVID CLARKE

VINDICATION

> 'Poets must not meddle with opinions. The poet
> who becomes a fighting man circumscribes his
> activity and coarsens his mind.'
> (John Butler Yeats: Early Memories. Cuala Prs.)
> Quoted in 'The Bell'

(To the memory of Charlie Donnelly)

He is astride the circus-ring and Grafton St.
His mellow arc-lamps watch the jeering stars.

Some Spanish maggots have, by now,
scavenged a skull of other eyes
that also saw the stars
framed in a crooked sky-light,
from shabby streets.
Saw man clawing their lives
from art-shop mountains,
the fragile cinders of good writing,
jail-striped skies.
Ears putrified now,
heard laughter strangled in a cough,
life staggering,
on shivering stairs.
Eyes saw, through the ultimate rifle-sight
a world worth singing.

Shout it then from shoddy roof-tops.
We have known worlds unsketched by Gertie,
unembossed by Cuala,
bigger, perhaps than bell-towers,
vivid, coarse, and vital worlds.
Our puny preaching songs will die
As we have died
But nothing is betrayed.

DONAGH MacDONAGH

CHARLES DONNELLY
Dead in Spain 1937

1.

Light in at the window and the uprisen
Hurry into an early grave, back to spider
And corrosive worm,
Who cast no shadow, who in the dimmest light
Are dimmer still. And he walks too
Lisping words in at my brain who spoke them once
In at my ear . . .
Is poetry feeling, or feeling poetry?

Such enterprise he had one land was not enough
For his ambition; and only death resolved him to be still,
To cease his far-seeking and lie still.
What he was seeking, whether death or another
Truth or emotion, but never glory,
I never knew. But death it was he found.

Dead and decayed this two years back
His worms are about their business,
Seek happily their own destiny in that foreign soil
Become the richest in two decades;
But moved not by his spirit, not led on
By the courageous mind that sought out what?
A pattern or a reason or something he called justice.

And in those years perjury has swayed the leaves,
Spoken out of the reeds and the mouths of children
And whispered even into the still pools of country villages.
And under the steel helmets death yawns out.

If this is human nature, nature must go . . .
But he has gone and nature lives and thrives
Fattening her bullocks for the coming fair;
And nature informs the loins as heretofore
While his flesh grows to earth and his smashed body
Forgets its lost humanity.

2.

Of what a quality is courage made
That he who gently walked our city street
Talking of poetry or philosophy,
Spinoza, Keats,
Should lie like any martyred soldier
His brave and fertile brain dried quite away
And the limbs that carried him from cradle to death's outpost
Growing down into a foreign clay.

Gone from amongst us and his life not half begun
Who had followed Jack-o'-Lantern truth and liberty
Where it led wavering from park-bed to prison cell
Into a strange land, dry misery,
And then into Spain's slaughter, sniper's aim
And his last shocked embrace of earth's lineaments.
Can I picture truly that swift end
Who see him dead with eye that still repents?

What end, what quietus can I see for him,
Who had the quality of life in every vein?
Life with its passion and poetry and its proud
Ignorance of eventual loss or gain . . .
This first fruit of our harvest, willing sacrifice
Upon the altar of his integrity,
Lost to us. Somewhere his death is charted,
A signature affixed to his brief history.

3.

They gave him a gun,
A trigger to pull that any peasant finger
Could have pulled as well, a barrel to keep sweet
That any eye from Valencia to Madrid
Could have looked through.
His body stopped a bullet and little else,
Stopped no tank or French 75
From crunching over roads of human bones . . .
His brain might have done that
But it has melted into Spanish soil;

But speaks into my brain in parody
Of the voice that was its servant,
And speaks only what it spoke before.
The intricate cells, the labyrinthine ways,
The multicoloured images that lurked and shone,
The dreams betrayed into expression
Melted into a red earth, richer for olive crop.

And through the pleasant European landscapes
The legions march; theodolite and map
Plan out the tactical approach, the gun emplacement,
The unencumbered field for cemetery.

4.

Bullets must search men out and teach them terror,
The whine of day and night raid make selective
The unoffending ear, and in the sun of midday
Jerk up the slumbering head, wake the reluctant brain,
Once more make fine lost instruments of caution
That throw men suddenly to the level floor
To hide from terror weakening the blood,
From shadows on the pale walls of the brain.

In the brave livery of war some die
Glad of another life given to dam
The rising flood, glad of the blood let loose
That will clog up advancing wheels,
Glad of the delicate brains ploughed through by lead.
These are the lucky ones who, gun in hand,
See consummated all their life and works.

Not so the aged whose life is memory,
Not so the boys who are too young to love,
To search life out or be searched out by death;
Not so the girls whose limbs are shot awry
By bursting shrapnel
Before they ever weakened in first love.

Bullets will search these out and teach them terror,
Will send them shivering to the earth's confines
To hide from men who are themselves, grown older.
The face behind the alarming mechanism of death
Is that of their own brother, their eyes are his,
The hand upon the trigger is their own.

Bullets will search us out and teach us terror,
Our faces grin behind the foreign gun.
The finger on the trigger is our own.